INTRODUCING
ISSUES WITH
OPPOSING
VIEWPOINTS®

Incarceration of Minors

Martin Gitlin, Book Editor

GREENHAVEN
PUBLISHING

Published in 2020 by Greenhaven Publishing, LLC
353 3rd Avenue, Suite 255, New York, NY 10010

Articles in Greenhaven Publishing anthologies are often edited for length to meet page requirements. In addition, original titles of these works are changed to clearly present the main thesis and to explicitly indicate the author's opinion. Every effort is made to ensure that Greenhaven Publishing accurately reflects the original intent of the authors. Every effort has been made to trace the owners of the copyrighted material.

Library of Congress Cataloging-in-Publication Data

Names: Gitlin, Marty, editor.
Title: Incarceration of minors / Martin Gitlin, book editor.
Description: New York : Greenhaven Publishing, [2020] | Series: Introducing
  issues with opposing viewpoints | Audience: Grade level 7–12. | Includes
  bibliographical references and index.
Identifiers: LCCN 2018055184| ISBN 9781534505704 (library bound) | ISBN
  9781534505711 (pbk.)
Subjects: LCSH: Juvenile justice, Administration of—United States. |
  Juvenile detention—United States. | Imprisonment—United States.
Classification: LCC HV9104 .I49 2020 | DDC 365/.420973—dc23
LC record available at https://lccn.loc.gov/2018055184

Manufactured in the United States of America

Website: http://greenhavenpublishing.com

Contents

Chapter 3: Does Age Matter?

Foreword

Indulging in a wide spectrum of ideas, beliefs, and perspectives is a critical cornerstone of democracy. After all, it is often debates over differences of opinion, such as whether to legalize abortion, how to treat prisoners, or when to enact the death penalty, that shape our society and drive it forward. Such diversity of thought is frequently regarded as the hallmark of a healthy and civilized culture. As the Reverend Clifford Schutjer of the First Congregational Church in Mansfield, Ohio, declared in a 2001 sermon, "Surrounding oneself with only like-minded people, restricting what we listen to or read only to what we find agreeable is irresponsible. Refusing to entertain doubts once we make up our minds is a subtle but deadly form of arrogance." With this advice in mind, Introducing Issues with Opposing Viewpoints books aim to open readers' minds to the critically divergent views that comprise our world's most important debates.

Introducing Issues with Opposing Viewpoints simplifies for students the enormous and often overwhelming mass of material now available via print and electronic media. Collected in every volume is an array of opinions that captures the essence of a particular controversy or topic. Introducing Issues with Opposing Viewpoints books embody the spirit of nineteenth-century journalist Charles A. Dana's axiom: "Fight for your opinions, but do not believe that they contain the whole truth, or the only truth." Absorbing such contrasting opinions teaches students to analyze the strength of an argument and compare it to its opposition. From this process readers can inform and strengthen their own opinions or be exposed to new information that will change their minds. Introducing Issues with Opposing Viewpoints is a mosaic of different voices. The authors are statesmen, pundits, academics, journalists, corporations, and ordinary people who have felt compelled to share their experiences and ideas in a public forum. Their words have been collected from newspapers, journals, books, speeches, interviews, and the internet, the fastest-growing body of opinionated material in the world.

Introducing Issues with Opposing Viewpoints shares many of the well-known features of its critically acclaimed parent series, Opposing

Viewpoints. The articles allow readers to absorb and compare divergent perspectives. Active reading questions preface each viewpoint, requiring students to approach the material thoughtfully and carefully. Photographs, charts, and graphs supplement each article. A thorough introduction provides readers with crucial background on an issue. An annotated bibliography points readers toward articles, books, and websites that contain additional information on the topic. An appendix of organizations to contact contains a wide variety of charities, nonprofit organizations, political groups, and private enterprises that each hold a position on the issue at hand. Finally, a comprehensive index allows readers to locate content quickly and efficiently.

Introducing Issues with Opposing Viewpoints is also significantly different from Opposing Viewpoints. As the series title implies, its presentation will help introduce students to the concept of opposing viewpoints and teach them to use this material to aid in critical writing and debate. The series' four-color, accessible format makes the books attractive and inviting to readers of all levels. In addition, each viewpoint has been carefully edited to maximize readers' understanding of the content. Short but thorough viewpoints capture the essence of an argument. A substantial, thought-provoking essay question placed at the end of each viewpoint asks students to further investigate the issues raised in the viewpoint, compare and contrast two authors' arguments, or consider how one might go about forming an opinion on the topic at hand. Each viewpoint contains sidebars that include at-a-glance information and handy statistics. A Facts About section located in the back of the book further supplies students with relevant facts and figures.

Following in the tradition of the Opposing Viewpoints series, Greenhaven Publishing continues to provide readers with invaluable exposure to the controversial issues that shape our world. As John Stuart Mill once wrote: "The only way in which a human being can make some approach to knowing the whole of a subject is by hearing what can be said about it by persons of every variety of opinion and studying all modes in which it can be looked at by every character of mind. No wise man ever acquired his wisdom in any mode but this." It is to this principle that Introducing Issues with Opposing Viewpoints books are dedicated.

Introduction

"Instead of nurturing responsible citizens, youth prisons risk systemically traumatizing youth and leaving them less able to find employment, have healthy relationships, get an education and lead productive lives."

—*Youth First Initiative national field director Mishi Faruqee*

It has been claimed with some merit that the benefit of one individual should not hinder the betterment of society. That argument has been used by those who favor the incarceration of minors for major crimes. Indeed, there is some truth to that contention. One could certainly assert that minors who are a danger to others should not be allowed to return to the streets.

But others argue that jailing youths accomplishes little more than turning them into career criminals and ensuring a greater chance of recidivism (relapse). They state that it is more productive to focus attention on treatment and rehabilitation of minors than to lock them up alongside adult convicts who provide a host of negative influences.

The latter notion has gained popularity in recent years. Jails throughout the United States are overcrowded. The US prison system costs taxpayers close to $40 billion annually. Many of those incarcerated launched criminal careers that could have been nipped in the bud at an early age. A large number never had the benefit of positive parental guidance. Activists and others who favor a change in the system believe that the least society can do for such wayward kids is provide them with a pathway to a better life, rather than send them to a prison where their most significant role models are often hardened criminals.

Advocates for the incarceration of minors counter that jails can and should provide treatment and rehabilitation in a contained environment. They believe that keeps law-abiding citizens safe until the young criminals have been rehabilitated enough to return to society. Some have also claimed that minors are better off having been taken from the streets, where committing crimes—often with fellow gang members—remains too tempting.

Those who rail against the incarceration of minors believe that the offenders receive more effective treatment outside the prison environment. After all, how can they be given the tools and confidence to become productive citizens when they must return to the company of career criminals? That is simply not an effective method of rehabilitation. Simply put, minors who commit crimes need to improve their self-image and self-respect, and that cannot be done within prison walls.

Another aspect of this debate is how it impacts society. The United States has the highest incarceration rate on the planet. Though it is home to only about 4 percent of the world population, the United States has more than one-fifth of its prisoners. The large number of minors in that equation simply weakens the country. It prevents many young people from gaining the potential to eventually join the workforce and become productive citizens. One can only speculate as to what positive impact an imprisoned minor could be making on the world if given an opportunity.

Replacing prison with counseling and strong job training for older minors has been suggested as a solution for instilling a positive self-image and a sense of right and wrong. Citing the recidivism rate (two-thirds of released prisoners are rearrested within three years, according to the National Institute of Justice), those who disagree with the option of incarceration believe that the current system has simply failed.

Emotion has played a huge role in promoting the current system. Millions of Americans learn about crimes committed by minors and say with conviction, "Lock them up and throw away the keys," instead of giving the question greater consideration. The issue is far more complex than that. Incarceration affects not only the individual youth but also many aspects of society. Millions of dollars must be spent to keep juveniles locked up—and for what purpose aside from keeping them off the streets? What if that money were spent on creating more effective treatment centers for minors who have committed major crimes? More thoughtful debate and legislation is necessary to emerge with better solutions for all concerned.

Those on the other side cite the victims of those crimes. They claim it is not justice when someone—even a minor—is able to escape jail after committing violence against another human being. Many loved ones of those harmed or even killed have demanded retribution, no matter the age of the perpetrator. They feel that anything less than a lengthy prison sentence is a mere slap on the wrist.

Many questions must be asked to bring both sides closer to working out a solution that benefits all. One question revolves around the age when a youth should be tried as an adult. Some believe it should be at least eighteen. But even those of that age who grow up in circumstances that promote criminality might not be old enough to know better.

What does seem certain is that communities and the nation as a whole must do a better job teaching kids at the youngest age possible how to live as good citizens in society. The debate regarding the incarceration of minors won't take on the same level of importance if a significantly larger number of kids learn the difference between right and wrong and gain enough self-confidence and self-respect to embark on a positive life path at an early age.

Until then, however, the debate will continue to rage. Should minors languish in prison despite evidence that return trips are inevitable? Or should society seek to rehabilitate them outside the prison walls and risk the dangers inherent in that system? The viewpoints in *Introducing Issues with Opposing Viewpoints: Incarceration of Minors* explore these and other related questions. It is important that we all work toward a solution that benefits our youth, communities, and society.

Chapter 1

What Is the Best Method for Rehabilitating Minors?

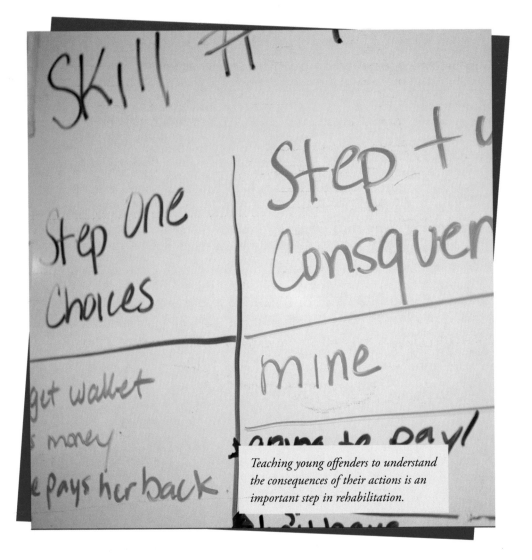

Teaching young offenders to understand the consequences of their actions is an important step in rehabilitation.

Viewpoint

1

Alternatives to Incarceration Make Economic Sense

"Members of the public are concerned about youth crime and want to reduce its incidence and are ready to support effective rehabilitative programs."

Alex Piquero and Laurence Steinberg

In the following excerpted viewpoint, Alex Piquero and Laurence Steinberg argue that public support for rehabilitation of serious juvenile offenders is much stronger than for punishment of those offenders. The authors cite approaches to reducing the overcrowding of jails. Among them are aggressive rehabilitation techniques for juveniles that keep them out of jails or seek to cut down on recidivism. The authors go on to explain the benefits of a wide range of models that could work in many communities and the positive public reaction to them. Piquero is a professor of criminology at the University of Texas at Dallas. Steinberg is a professor of psychology at Temple University.

"Rehabilitation Versus Incarceration of Juvenile Offenders: Public Preferences in Four Models for Change States," by Alex Piquero and Laurence Steinberg, Elsevier, January 1, 2008. Reprinted by permission.

AS YOU READ, CONSIDER THE FOLLOWING QUESTIONS:
1. Were survey participants more willing to pay for rehabilitation or punishment?
2. In which state were participants willing to pay the most for rehabilitation rather than punishment?
3. Whose view do the authors say they are challenging?

An assessment of the public's support for various responses to juvenile offending is important because policy makers often justify expenditures for punitive juvenile justice reforms on the basis of popular demand. Punitive responses to juvenile crime (e.g., the incarceration of juvenile offenders in correctional facilities) are far more expensive and often less effective than less harsh alternatives (e.g., providing juvenile offenders rehabilitative services in community settings). If politicians' misreading of public sentiment has led to the adoption of more expensive policy alternatives than the public actually wants, tax dollars are likely being wasted on policies that are costly and possibly ineffective, and that also may be less popular than is widely assumed.

[...]

Results

As Figures 1 and 2 indicate, across the sample as a whole (that is, with data from all four states combined), the public clearly favors rehabilitation over punishment as a response to serious juvenile offending. More respondents are willing to pay for additional rehabilitation than for additional punishment, and the average amount in additional annual taxes that respondents are willing to pay for rehabilitation is almost 20% greater than it is for incarceration ($98.49 versus $84.52). Conversely, significantly more respondents are unwilling to pay for additional incarceration (39 percent) than are unwilling to pay for added rehabilitation (29 percent). It is quite clear that the public supports rehabilitation and is willing to pay for it.

This general pattern holds in three of the four Models for Change sites: Pennsylvania, Washington and Illinois. In Pennsylvania, the

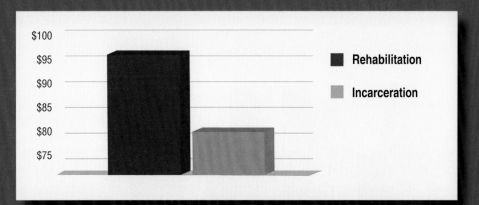

Figure 1. Average Annual Amount of Additional Taxes the Public Would Be Willing to Pay for Rehabilitation or Incarceration

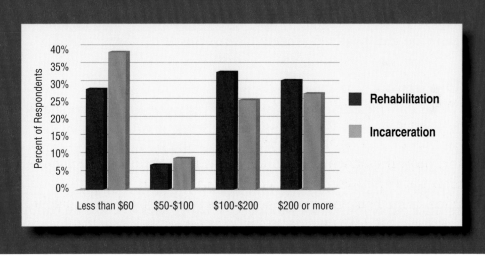

Figure 2. Annual Amount of Additional Taxes the Public Would Be Willing to Pay for Rehabilitation or Incarceration

public is willing to pay 18% more for rehabilitation than punishment ($98 versus $83). In Washington, the public is willing to pay 29% more ($102 versus $79). And in Illinois, the public is willing to pay 36% more for rehabilitation than punishment ($100 versus $73

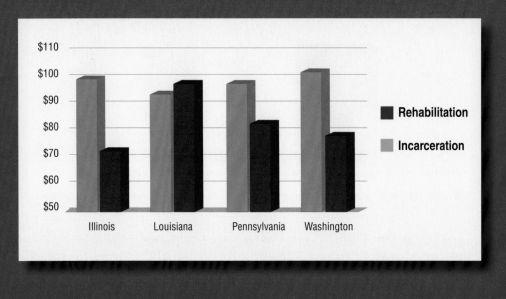

Figure 3. Average Annual Amount of Additional Taxes the Public Would Be Willing to Pay for Rehabilitation or Incarceration

annually). In Louisiana, the amounts for rehabilitation and punishment are statistically equivalent ($94 versus $98). (See Figure 3)

Discussion

When informed that rehabilitation is as effective as incarceration (in fact, the former is more effective), the public is willing to pay nearly 20 percent more in additional taxes annually for programs that offer rehabilitative services to serious juvenile offenders than for longer periods of incarceration. We find this for the sample as a whole, and in three out of four of the Models for Change sites (the sole exception is Louisiana).

These results are consistent with public opinion surveys in general, which usually find more public support for rehabilitation than politicians may believe is the case. The added value of the present survey is that this general trend is found using a methodology that is thought to more accurately gauge public support for various policy alternatives than conventional polling.

Rehabilitation can include pet therapy to aid in exploration of responsibility, caring, and empathy.

One criticism of this approach to assessing public opinion is that the actual dollar amounts generated through the method may not be accurate, because respondents are forced to pick among predetermined responses. Some individuals who indicate a willingness to pay $200 in additional taxes may in fact be willing to pay even more, but because we did not press beyond this amount, we do not know how large this group is, nor do we know how responses would have differed had we used different dollar amounts to anchor the response categories. Moreover, because the respondents know they are answering a hypothetical question, their responses may differ from what they would say if a genuine referendum were held.

The absolute dollar amounts are less important than the relative amounts, however. Although the true dollar amount that taxpayers are willing to pay for either policy may be uncertain, what is certainly clear is that participants are willing to pay more for rehabilitation than for incarceration if each delivers the same result. This finding, together with evidence that incarceration is substantially more costly than rehabilitation (at least five times more costly, according to some estimates), supports the conclusion that the returns per dollar spent on rehabilitation are a better value than the returns on incarceration. Support for rehabilitation would likely be even stronger if respondents were told that at least five offenders can be provided with services for the same price as incarcerating just one of them.

Our survey challenges the view held by many politicians and the media that the public opposes rehabilitation and favors incarceration of young offenders. According to conventional wisdom, the driving force behind the punitive reforms in recent years has been the public demand for tough juvenile justice policies, and politicians frequently point to public outrage at serious juvenile crime as justification for sweeping legislative reforms.

We believe, instead, that members of the public are concerned about youth crime and want to reduce its incidence and are ready to support effective rehabilitative programs as a means of accomplishing that end—indeed favoring rehabilitation to imposing more punishment through longer sentences. Our findings offer encouragement to lawmakers who are uncomfortable with the recent trend toward punitive juvenile justice policies and would like to initiate more moderate reforms.

The high cost of punitive sentencing has become a consideration in the public debate—long sentences translate into more prison space, more staff and generally higher operating costs. Cost-conscious legislatures may become disenchanted with punitive juvenile justice policies on economic grounds and pursue policies that place greater emphasis on rehabilitation and early childhood prevention. If so, they may be reassured, on the basis of our findings, that the public will support this move.

EVALUATING THE AUTHORS' ARGUMENTS:

Do the viewpoint authors make sound economic arguments in favor of rehabilitation over imprisonment of juvenile offenders? How does focusing on economics help or hurt their argument?

Minimizing Juvenile Delinquency Starts with a Strong Family

Mayra Aguilera

"Having a support system at home can encourage a teen to finish school, find a job and get involved with positive activities."

In the following viewpoint, Mayra Aguilera argues that the current justice system in the United States betrays its youth by emphasizing prison sentences that create career criminals over rehabilitation that works to turn young lawbreakers into responsible and productive citizens. She believes that association with hardened criminals in prisons has a greatly negative effect on minors—the opposite effect of rehabilitation. The author further claims that treatment for alcohol and drugs can also turn the lives of minors around more effectively than prison sentences. Aguilera is a graduate student in educational counseling at San Jose State University.

"More Treatment, Better Treatment & Beyond Treatment," by Mayra Aguilera, November 25, 2012. Reprinted by permission.

AS YOU READ, CONSIDER THE FOLLOWING QUESTIONS:
1. Based on the viewpoint, do you believe that imprisoning minors has not worked?
2. Are prisons to blame for turning some youths into career criminals?
3. How has a lack of support at home increased the chance for recidivism among youths released from jail?

Many people are asking what the future holds for our juvenile justice system and our growing youth? As we are currently dealing with a system that for many years has placed a strong emphasis on reactive punishment for criminal delinquents such as incarcerating our youth in adult prisons and "scaring them straight" with harsh punishments. We have seen that these types of extreme measures do not work for adolescents who are out in the community committing crimes, or those who are already caught up in the criminal justice system. These teens are actually learning to become tougher in these institutions and are getting the chance to associate with more serious offenders. What we need to see in the future of the juvenile justice system is for the system as a whole to seek a brighter future and seek to change in all aspects of so that teens get the help they need and communities are safer.

To do that, judges, probation officers, substance abuse treatment professionals, and community members have to work together to help out the children that have been consumed by this system. Developing a local leadership where all of these administrators can come together and work on establishing a common goal in which will retain a positive reaction to our delinquent youth is an idea that can, if properly and thoroughly executed, change the life of many within the community. Judges can promote change within the judicial system that can affect the way all teens seen by the court are handled and their standing in the community can change public attitudes towards youth in the trouble with the law. The treatment professionals such as counselors and probation officers are the ones who should be guiding young people through the juvenile justice system and provide assistance to families to set a healthy lifestyle,

Group rehabilitation may be more effective than incarceration for some juvenile offenders.

therefore serving as a central influence when it comes to setting these adolescents in the right path. Members of community also need to become involved in this process to assist as support and engage these adolescents in positive activities post treatment.

We know that many teens in America are experimenting with alcohol and drugs, and research shows that teens with substance abuse problems are more likely to break the law, behave violently, or drop out of school. According to national data, almost two million young people ages 12 to 17 need treatment for substance abuse or dependence, but only one in 10 will get treated (*Reclaiming Futures*, 2012). That's unfortunate, because effective adolescent substance abuse treatment can help teens stay out of trouble, make our communities safer, and save money. Young people need to be held accountable when they break the law, but unless they receive treatment when they have a substance abuse problem that helped them get in trouble in the first place, they will usually find themselves back in juvenile court again and again.

Practitioner recommendations for improving the effectiveness of the juvenile justice system generally focused on providing adequate resources including qualified staff and financial resources for training, staff development, and programs and services. Administering juvenile justice in a collaborative manner, using a range of sanctions to provide meaningful and effective consequences, focusing on prevention and interventions to address juveniles' unique needs, and developing policies and practices based on evidence and practitioner input represented other notable respondent recommendations (Willison, Mears, & Butts, 2010).

So what do teens in the juvenile justice system need? They need more treatment, better treatment and beyond treatment. In order for America to produce law-abiding children and adolescents we must focus on prevention and early intervention with an emphasis on treatment and programs. The local juvenile justice systems must do a better job of identifying teens that need treatment, and assess their individual needs by helping them implement high-quality, validated screening and assessment tools and placing them in the proper treatment.

It's important to act quickly when a teen is ready to participate in treatment—those windows of opportunity close quickly. Interning with the local school district for the past three months has taught me that adolescents change their mind about treatment about three times in the same week so we must quickly take advantage of their desire to change.

Almost every young person who appears in front of a juvenile court eventually returns home, and to be able to remain crime-free after probation these teens need mentors and care from the adults in their lives. Having a support system at home can encourage a teen to finish school, find a job and get involved with positive activities around their community. We must believe that our children can change and no matter what role someone plays in the community we should all be responsible for seeking change in the lives of our future.

References

Investing in Reclaiming Futures: A Guide for Public Agencies, Policymakers, and Foundations. (2012). *Reclaiming Futures*. Retrieved November 23, 2012, from http://www
.reclaimingfutures.org/sites/default/files/main_documents/Investing_in_RF_FINAL
.pdf

Willison, J. B., Mears, D. P., & Butts, J. A. (2010). *Past, present, and future of juvenile justice assessing the policy options (APO): final report*. Washington, D.C.: Urban Institute.

Weissberg, Roger P., Karol L. Kumpfer, and Martin E. P. Seligman. "Prevention That Works For Children And Youth: An Introduction." *American Psychologist* 58.6–7 (2003): 425–432. PsycARTICLES. Web. 8 Nov. 2012.

EVALUATING THE AUTHOR'S ARGUMENTS:

Viewpoint author Mayra Aguilera argues that family-based programs and focus on the home can prevent many cases of childhood delinquency. How does the author suggest that child development impacts our society when it comes to criminal behavior?

Viewpoint

3

The United States Incarcerates Juveniles at a Much Higher Rate than Other Nations

"Incarcerating juveniles, at tremendous cost, serves to reduce their educational attainment and increase the probability of incarceration as an adult."

Anna Aizer and Joseph Doyle

In the following viewpoint, Anna Aizer and Joseph Doyle argue that the inability of imprisoned youths to maximize their academic and social potential comes at a cost to a society to which they could be contributing if the system embraced an approach that stressed rehabilitation. The authors have explored the economic impact of juvenile incarceration but also address the human side of the problem in making the case that both are inextricably linked. Ultimately, they express a sense of optimism that lawmakers and courts have come to the same conclusions. Aizer is an associate professor of economics at Brown University. Doyle is a professor of applied economics at MIT.

"What Is the Long-Term Impact of Incarcerating Juveniles?" by Anna Aizer and Joseph Doyle, VoxEU.org, July 16, 2013. Reprinted by permission. Available at: https://voxeu.org/article/what-long-term-impact-incarcerating-juveniles.

AS YOU READ, CONSIDER THE FOLLOWING QUESTIONS:
1. How has the large number of minors in prison negatively impacted the American economy?
2. Why is the youth incarceration rate so much higher in the United States than in other countries?
3. Has the United States made progress since the turn of the century with this problem?

The US imprisons more young people at a higher rate than any other nation. This column argues that, at a tremendous cost, incarcerating juveniles only serves to reduce their educational attainment and increase the probability of incarceration as an adult. New research suggests that using the numerous available alternatives will probably not only save the US money in the short run—as well as giving juvenile criminals better prospects in the future—but will also reduce future crime and thus future expenditures in the long run.

The US incarcerates juveniles at a much higher rate than other nations. It spends some $6 billion per year on juvenile corrections (see Figure 1 from Mendel 2011). In fact, on any given day, there are over 70,000 juveniles in custody in the US (OJJDP 2011) with an average (direct) cost of $88,000 per juvenile per year.

Despite such high rates and the associated direct costs, little is known about the impact of incarcerating juveniles on their long-term outcomes such as educational attainment and the likelihood of further offenses as an adult. On the one hand, incarceration at an early age might serve to reduce future criminal activity by making the cost of later incarceration more salient. On the other hand, incarceration during adolescence may interrupt human and social capital accumulation at a critical moment leading to reduced future wages in the legal sector and greater criminal activity (Becker 1968).

The lack of existing empirical work on this topic is due to two main factors:

- First, estimation is complicated by the fact that juveniles who are incarcerated differ from those who are not. They have likely

US prisons are full of older inmates, many of whom are repeat offenders, who drain resources and taxpayer money.

committed more serious crimes, their background may be more disadvantaged, and as a result their underlying propensity to drop out of school and commit a crime in the future may be higher than that of juveniles who were not committed. Unfortunately, it is difficult to control for these confounding factors that tend to overstate the effects of juvenile incarceration on the propensity to drop out of high school or become incarcerated as an adult.

- A second complicating factor is the dearth of data that includes information on juvenile incarceration and long-term outcomes. Survey data is generally insufficient to estimate the impact of juvenile incarceration on future outcomes because few survey respondents would have spent time in juvenile detention as a youth and there is underreporting of criminal activity and incarceration. In the observational studies that have been conducted, De Li (1999), Tanner et al. (1999) and Sweeten (2006) find that juvenile incarceration is correlated with a higher likelihood of dropping out of high school. Hjalmarsson (2008) also finds such effects when comparing siblings, although the results apply to a small number of households.

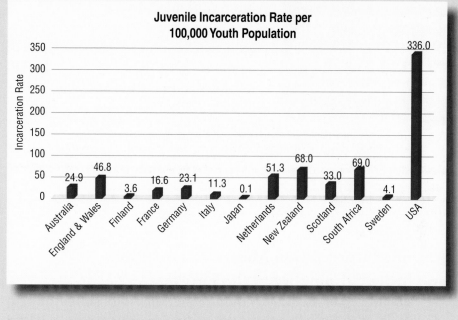

Figure 1. Youth Incarceration Rate in the US Versus Other Nations

Juvenile Incarceration Rate per 100,000 Youth Population

Source: Hazel, Neal, *Cross-National Comparison of Youth Justice*, London: Youth Justice Board, 2008.

New Research

In a recent paper, we tested which of the two potential effects of juvenile incarceration dominates by examining empirically how incarceration as a juvenile influences high school completion—a partial measure of social and human capital formation—and the likelihood of incarceration later in life (Aizer and Doyle 2013).

To address the first complicating factor we exploit the random assignment of cases to judges who vary in their sentencing.

Specifically, we examine the outcomes of juveniles who are very similar based on their observable characteristics (same age, race, crime, and neighbourhood) but who by chance are assigned to judges who differ in their sentencing severity. In this way, we can compare the outcomes of two identical (or near identical) juveniles, one of whom, by virtue of random assignment to a "stricter" judge, is incarcerated and one of whom, by virtue of assignment to a more "lenient" judge, is not. With this strategy we address the issue of negative selection into juvenile incarceration.

Second, we do not use survey data, but rather a unique source of linked administrative data for over 35,000 juveniles over ten years who came before a juvenile court in Chicago, Illinois.

These data were linked to both public-school data for the same city and adult-incarceration data for the same state to investigate effects of juvenile incarceration on high-school completion and adult imprisonment.

Juvenile Incarceration Means Worse Grades and More Criminality in the Future

We find that juvenile incarceration reduces the probability of high school completion and increases the probability of incarceration later in life. While some of this relationship reflects omitted variables (as described above), even when we control for potential confounding factors using random assignment to judges, the relationships remain strong. In regressions with minimal controls, those incarcerated as a juvenile are 39 percentage points less likely to graduate from high school and are 41 percentage points more likely to have entered adult prison by age 25 compared with other public school students from the same neighbourhood. Once we include demographic controls, limit our comparison group to juveniles charged with a crime in court but not incarcerated, and exploit random assignment to judges, juvenile incarceration is estimated to decrease high school graduation by 13 percentage points and increase adult incarceration by 22 percentage points. The results, while smaller than the initial results, remain large and suggest substantial negative effects of juvenile incarceration on long-term outcomes.

Conclusions

Our results suggest that incarcerating juveniles, at tremendous cost, serves to reduce their educational attainment and increase the probability of incarceration as an adult. Interestingly, after years of steady increases in juvenile incarceration, in the past decade, juvenile incarceration has started to decline.

- Nationally, juvenile incarceration has dropped 32% from 2002 to the present (National Juvenile Justice Network 2013).
- This is driven by both falling rates of crime and by concerted efforts on the part of roughly ten (of the largest) states to reduce expenditures on juvenile incarceration by substituting to less costly community-based alternatives.

This trend extends to Chicago which has more alternatives to incarceration now than it did when many of the subjects were being sentenced in the early 1990s.

- The evidence presented here suggests that shifting to such alternatives will likely not only save the states money in the short run, but also reduce future crime and thus expenditures on corrections in the long run.

Whether this trend of reductions in rates of juvenile incarceration will continue, however, is not clear. The New York City School Justice Partnership Task Force refers to the recent development of a "school-to-prison pipeline" whereby students involved in relatively minor infractions are increasingly likely to be arrested. Again the evidence presented here suggests that policies or practices putting more juveniles in detention are likely to have high short and long-term costs.

References

Aizer, A and J J Doyle Jr (2013), "Juvenile Incarceration, Human Capital and Future Crime: Evidence from Randomly-Assigned Judges," NBER Working Paper, 19102, available at.

Becker, G (1968), "Crime and Punishment: An Economic Approach," *Journal of Political Economy* 76, 169–217.

De Li, S (1999), "Legal Sanctions and Youths' Status Achievement: A Longitudinal Study," *Justice Quarterly* 16, 377–401.

Hazel, N (2008), "Cross-National Comparison of Youth Justice," London, Youth Justice Board for England and Wales.

Hjalmarsson, R (2008), "Criminal Justice Involvement and High School Completion," *Journal of Urban Economics* 63: 613–630.

Mendel, R A (2011), "No Place for Kids: The Case for Reducing Juvenile Incarceration," Baltimore, The Annie E Casey Foundation.

National Juvenile Justice Network and the Texas Public Policy Foundation (2013), "The Comeback States: Reducing youth incarceration in the US" in The New York City School Justice Partnership Task Force, "Keeping Kids in School and Out of Court."

Office of Juvenile Justice and Delinquency Prevention (2011), "Census of Juveniles in Residential Placement 2010," Washington, DC, OJJDP.

Sweeten, G (2006), "Who Will Graduate? Disruption of High School Education by Arrest and Court Involvement," *Justice Quarterly* 23, 462–480.

Tanner, J, S Davies and B O'Grady (1999), "Whatever Happened to Yesterday's Rebels? Longitudinal Effects of Youth Delinquency on Education and Employment," *Social Problems* 46, 250–274.

EVALUATING THE AUTHORS' ARGUMENTS:

The viewpoint authors used statistical data to make the claim that locking up juveniles greatly hinders their educational opportunities. Was this use of data effective? What other ways of supporting their argument might have been more or less effective?

Sweden Has a Radical Solution to Crime

"The implication in the Swedish model is that sentenced individuals are still primarily regarded as people with needs."

Erwin James

In the following viewpoint, Erwin James argues that Sweden's treatment and rehabilitation of juvenile offenders is a resounding success in comparison to the failures of the American and British systems. The author expresses his feeling that rather than youths being treating like they are beyond repair, they should be viewed as needful and desirous of turning their lives around. He believes youths require tough love and assistance, as is achieved in Sweden's model of juvenile justice. James is a columnist for the *Guardian*. He served 20 years of a life sentence in prison.

AS YOU READ, CONSIDER THE FOLLOWING QUESTIONS:
1. Why might one argue that the Swedish model of rehabilitation would not work in the United States?
2. Why could such a model be successful in the United States?
3. How does Sweden work to prevent criminality among its youth?

"Prison Is Not for Punishment in Sweden. We Get People into Better Shape," by Erwin James, Guardian News and Media Limited, November 26, 2014. Reprinted by permission.

In Sweden, prison cells are quite different from US prison cells.

O ur role is not to punish. The punishment is the prison sentence: they have been deprived of their freedom. The punishment is that they are with us," says Nils Öberg, director-general of Sweden's prison and probation service.

Öberg, 54, is giving the annual Longford lecture on penal reform in London tomorrow, where he will explain how, in stark contrast to the UK, Sweden is closing prisons and reducing the prison population.

Since 2004, Swedish prisoner numbers have fallen from 5,722 to 4,500 out of a population of 9.5 million, and last year four of the country's 56 prisons were closed and parts of other jails mothballed. In contrast, the prison population in England and Wales is 85,000 out of a population of 57 million.

With reoffending rates at about 40%—less than half of those in the UK and most other European countries—does he attribute this success to the country's effective policies on prisoner rehabilitation? "We obviously believe that it is part of the explanation; we hope we are doing something right. But it's going to be very difficult to prove that scientifically. We are increasing our efforts all the time," he says.

Last year a "national client survey" of several thousand Swedish prisoners was undertaken in order to identify the issues that have affected their criminal behaviour. "The survey did not bring up any surprises, but it gave us confirmation of what we have learned from experience—that it is not one problem that our clients face, but two or more, sometimes as many as seven or eight different ones, including perhaps drugs, alcohol and psychiatric problems. And these problems did not just appear over-night. These are things that have developed over years. Most of the sentences in this country are relatively short. The window of opportunity that we have to make a change is very small, so we need to start from day one. Our strategy is to cover the whole range of problems, not just the one problem."

Unlike England and Wales, where since 2004 anyone convicted by the courts is categorised as an offender, the implication in the Swedish model is that sentenced individuals are still primarily regarded as people with needs, to be assisted and helped. As well as having rehabilitation at the heart of its penal policy, the other huge difference between the Swedish and UK approaches is the role of politicians.

Chris Grayling, the justice secretary, has recently introduced measures that amount to "a ramped-up political emphasis on punishment rather than real rehabilitation" in prison regimes, according to Juliet Lyon, director of the Prison Reform Trust. These include forcing prisoners to wear uniform, banning books being sent to prisoners, and turning off cell lights at 10.30pm in young offender institutions.

Öberg says: "A politician who tried something like that in Sweden would be thrown out of office. It would be a breach of our constitution—in our system that is the forbidden area. When we exercise authority over individuals, a politician cannot interfere with the administration process. In reality, there is a dialogue—politicians will tell me and my colleagues what they expect and we will do our best to achieve those goals. We have a very clear division of labour between the government and public administration.

"An individual politician cannot interfere with the running of our business. The government sets goals in a yearly letter of intent, and then the responsibility for the work is entirely ours."

But what about public opinion in Sweden? Is there less desire for retribution than in the UK? "There is a lot of anger among the Swedish public when it comes to crime and criminals," says Öberg. "But, regardless of what public opinion may be at any one time, whatever you do in the justice sector, you have to take a long-term perspective. You cannot try something one day and then change it to something else the next day—that would be completely useless. The system in our sector is set up to implement long-term strategies and stick to them."

He adds, however, that the country's well-educated population appreciates that almost all prisoners will return to society. "So when you go into a political dialogue, there is a fair amount of understanding that the more we can do during this small window of opportunity when people are deprived of their liberty, the better it will be in the long run."

Is he hoping his Longford lecture will provide some helpful advice that may assist the UK government with its prison difficulties, ranging from overcrowding, staff shortages and a 69% increase last year in self-inflicted death?

"I'm very excited to be giving the lecture. But I will be very careful about giving anybody any advice. We can try to share our experiences and perhaps inspire each other a little bit, recognising that the preconditions for carrying out our work are very, very different.

"My ambition is to try to tell a story about how we have come to the conclusions that we have, and explain why we have made the choices that we have made. It has to do with whether you decide to use prison as your first option or as a last resort, and what you want your probation system to achieve. Some people have to be incarcerated, but it has to be a goal to get them back out into society in better shape than they were when they came in."

EVALUATING THE AUTHOR'S ARGUMENTS:

How does viewpoint author Erwin James explain the vast differences between the outcomes of the Swedish and British systems of juvenile justice? Does the comparison serve to bolster his argument?

Viewpoint

5

Low-Risk Offenders Should Have Minimal Contact with High-Risk Offenders

"Longer sentences are associated with higher rates of re-offending. When prisoners return to their communities ... the problems multiply."

Andrew Day

In the following viewpoint, Andrew Day argues the importance of rehabilitating youths effectively enough that they do not return to a life of crime and become yet more victims of recidivism. Day cites the ineffectiveness of prisons in transforming young offenders into law-abiding and respectful citizens with positive goals and aspirations. He believes the trend toward tougher sentencing in his home country of Australia has had a negative effect. The same can be argued about the American system, which has also failed. Day is a professor of psychology at Deakin University in Australia.

AS YOU READ, CONSIDER THE FOLLOWING QUESTIONS:
1. Does early recidivism make it harder for youths to ever rehabilitate?
2. What can Americans learn from the problems in Australia's system?
3. Are there parallels between the treatment of minors from culturally disadvantaged backgrounds in Australia and the United States?

Although criminal justice agencies in Australia have, in recent years, adopted an increasingly "get tough" approach, responses to crime that rely on punishment alone have failed to make our communities safer. Instead, they have produced an expanding prison system. This has the potential to do more harm than good and places considerable strain on government budgets.

Increasing prison sentences does little to deter criminal behaviour. Longer sentences are associated with higher rates of re-offending. When prisoners return to their communities, as the vast majority inevitably do, the problems multiply.

Exposing the Limitations of Punishment

In this context, it becomes important to think carefully about public policy responses that aim to punish and deter offenders. Psychologists have been studying punishment under well-controlled laboratory conditions with both animals and humans for nearly 100 years. Its effectiveness in promoting short-term behavioural change, or even in suppressing negative behaviour, depends on rather specific conditions being in place.

For punishment to work it has to be predictable. Punishment also has to be applied at maximum intensity to work, or else tolerance and temporary effects result. Yet applying very intense levels of punishment for many offences goes against our sense of justice and fairness.

The threat of punishment, no matter how severe, will not deter anyone who believes they can get away with it. It will also not deter those who are too overcome by emotion or disordered thinking to care about the consequences of their behaviour.

Effective rehabilitation programs include job training and teaching of trades to prepare offenders to be productive members of society.

Punishment also has to be immediate. Delayed punishment provides opportunities for other behaviours to be reinforced. In reality, it often takes months—if not years—for someone to be apprehended, appear in court and be sentenced.

Working Towards More Effective Rehabilitation

Many of the conditions required for punishment to be effective will not exist in any justice system. It follows that policies and programmes that focus on rehabilitating offenders will have a greater chance of success in preventing crime and improving community safety.

The origins of offender rehabilitation in Australia can be traced back to the early penal colonies and, in particular, to the work of Alexander Maconochie, a prison governor on Norfolk Island in 1840. Maconochie introduced the idea of indeterminate rather than fixed sentences, implemented a system of rehabilitation in which good behaviour counted towards prisoners' early release, and advocated a system of aftercare and community resettlement.

Maconochie's ideas built on those of the great social reformers of 18th-century Britain, notably Quakers such as John Howard and Elizabeth Fry. They were among the first to try to change prisons from what they called "institutions of deep despair and cruel punishment" to places that were more humane and had the potential to reform prisoners' lives.

These days, though, offender rehabilitation is often thought about in terms of psychological treatment. We can chart the rise of current programmes according to the broad traditions of psychodynamic psychotherapy, behaviour modification and behaviour therapy and, more recently, the cognitive-behavioural and cognitive approaches that characterise contemporary practice.

The earliest therapeutic work in the psychoanalytic tradition saw delinquent behaviour as the product of a failure in psychological development. It was thought this could be addressed through gaining insight into the causes of offending. A wide range of group and milieu therapies were developed for use with offenders, including group counselling and psychodrama.

In the 1980s, more behavioural methods—such as token economies, contingency management programmes and "time out"—replaced psychotherapy.

There are good grounds to develop standardised incentive models in Australia's prisons. Community-style therapeutic programmes for prisoners with substance use problems in Victoria, NSW and the ACT represent substantial advances in practice.

These programmes take advantage of the significant therapeutic opportunities that arise by looking closely at prisoners' social functioning and day-to-day interactions. They actively encourage offenders to assume responsibility not only for their own behaviour, but for that of others.

However, rehabilitation today is almost always associated with cognitive-behavioural therapy. This targets a relatively narrow range of crime-producing (or "criminogenic") needs, including pro-criminal attitudes—those thoughts, values and sentiments that support criminal conduct. Programmes also dedicate a lot of time to trying to change personality traits, such as low self-control, hostility, pleasure- or thrill-seeking and lack of empathy.

Not everyone can be successfully treated. Substantial evidence now exists, though, to suggest that this type of approach does produce socially significant reductions in re-offending.

Essential Steps in Making Corrections Policy Work

The challenges lie in ensuring that the right programmes are delivered to the right people at the right time.

First, it is important that low-risk offenders have minimal contact with higher-risk offenders. Extended contact is only likely to increase their risk of recidivism. This has implications for prisoner case management, prison design and for the courts.

Courts have the power to divert low-risk offenders from prison and thus minimise contact with more entrenched offenders. Related to this is the need to develop effective systems of community-based rehabilitation, leaving prisons for the most dangerous and highest-risk offenders.

Second, concerted efforts are required to develop innovative programmes for those who identify with Aboriginal or Torres Strait Islander cultural backgrounds. They are grossly over-represented across all levels of the criminal justice system.

Third, staff need to be properly selected, trained, supervised and resourced to deliver the highest-quality rehabilitation services to the most complex and challenging people.

Finally, it is important to demonstrate that programmes actually make offenders better, not worse. The types of evaluation that are needed to attribute positive change to programme completion are complex, require large numbers of participants and cross-jurisdictional collaboration. A national approach to programme evaluation is sorely needed.

This is not to suggest that criminal behaviour shouldn't be punished—only that we should not rely on punishment by itself to change behaviour. We need to create a true system of rehabilitation that can enhance the corrective impact of punishment-based approaches.

It also doesn't mean that punishment never works. It may work reasonably well with some people—perhaps those who are future-oriented, have good self-monitoring and regulation skills, and who can make the connection between their behaviour and negative consequences months later.

Unfortunately, many people in prison simply aren't like this. The challenge, then, is two-fold: to find ways to make punishment more effective and to tackle the causes of offending through high-quality rehabilitation.

Correctional services often get little credit for their efforts. They are widely criticised when things go wrong. However, their efforts to rehabilitate offenders are not only sensible, but also cost-efficient and practical.

We need to support efforts to create a true system of rehabilitation. Such a system will be comprehensive, coherent and internally consistent in applying evidence-based practice at all levels.

EVALUATING THE AUTHOR'S ARGUMENTS:

How does viewpoint author Andrew Day use history to make a point about the benefits of rehabilitation over imprisonment? His arguments in favor of rehabilitation and individually based sentencing extend back to the nineteenth century.

Chapter 2

What Are Minors Doing in Major Prisons?

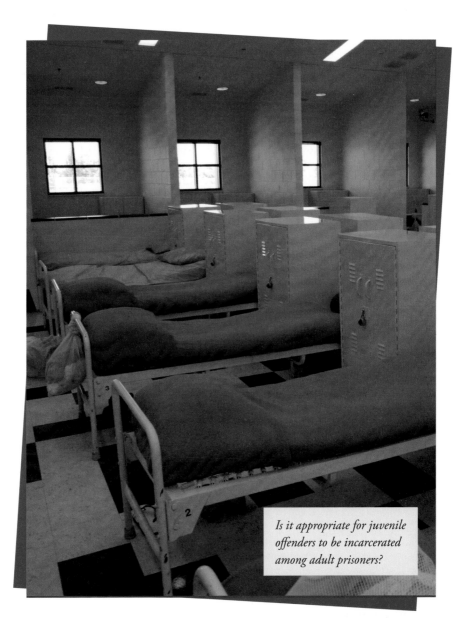

Is it appropriate for juvenile offenders to be incarcerated among adult prisoners?

Viewpoint

1

More States Are Keeping Juveniles Out of the Adult System

Caitlin Curley

"Young people who go through the adult system are 34 percent more likely than those in the juvenile system to be re-arrested."

In the following viewpoint, Caitlin Curley argues that placing youths in adult prisons and exposing them to hardened criminals makes it far more difficult for young prisoners to emerge from custody rehabilitated and prepared to become productive members of society. Too often, the result is that they are back on the street committing crimes, leading to an unacceptable rate of recidivism. The author espouses a system that allows minors to make major positive changes in their lives. Curley was a crime reporter at the *Rocky Mountain Collegian*.

AS YOU READ, CONSIDER THE FOLLOWING QUESTIONS:
1. How has the placement of minors in adult prisons weakened opportunities for rehabilitation?
2. Have states done enough to reduce the number of youths tried as adults?
3. Are there certain crimes that should result in minors being prosecuted as adults?

"Juveniles Tried as Adults: What Happens When Children Go to Prison," by Caitlin Curley, GenFKD, November 11, 2016. Reprinted by permission.

Many incarcerated minors don't have the skills to adapt to life outside bars. This can lead to a cycle of repeat arrests and imprisonment.

Most juveniles tried as adults, and/or placed in adult facilities, are being denied education and subjected to various dangers, both of which can lead to permanent setbacks and high rates of recidivism.

The majority of states have already started passing reforms to make it more difficult to prosecute juveniles as adults, but there is a long way to go.

Juveniles in the Adult System

Following the tough on crime era, the practice of trying youth as adults has become much more common in recent years. Between 1990 and 2010, the number of juveniles in adult jails went up by nearly 230 percent.

Around 250,000 youth are tried, sentenced or incarcerated as adults in the United States every year. On any given day, around 10,000 juveniles are housed in adult jails and prisons—7,500 in jails and 2,700 in prisons, respectively.

Of the juveniles held in adult jails, most of them are awaiting trial, as 39 states permit or require that youth charged as adults be held in an adult jail before they are tried. Though as many as a half of them will not be convicted or will be sent back to the juvenile justice system, most will have spent at least one month in the adult jail, and one in five of them will have spent over six months there.

The juveniles held in adult prisons have been convicted as adults; the laws and standards of this practice vary wildly by state. The majority of youth prosecuted in adult court are charged with nonviolent offenses.

Federal law states that youth transferred from juvenile facilities to the adult system must be separated by sight and sound from adult inmates, but many states have either refused to comply with these laws (and forfeited federal grant money) or stated that they will comply only to stall on progress.

A Lack of Education

There are numerous federal and state laws granting all juveniles the right to education, which apply to youth in correctional facilities. However, many youth housed in adult facilities do not have access to any education. A 2005 survey of adult facilities found that 40 percent of the jails and prisons had no educational services at all.

Additionally, the Individuals with Disabilities Act requires that incarcerated youth with learning disabilities and other mental disorders be granted education that serves individual needs and prepares students for college, employment and independent living. Yet, that same survey found that only 11 percent of correctional facilities provided special education services and an even smaller 7 percent actually provided vocational training.

The Other Dangers

The issue of course goes beyond a denial of education and other much-needed rehabilitative services. Youth in the adult system are at extreme risk for sexual victimization, more than "any other group of incarcerated persons," according to the National Prison Rape Elimination Commission. And the Prison Rape Elimination Act of 2003 asserted that children are five times more likely to be sexually assaulted in adult prisons than in juvenile facilities, often within the first 48 hours of their incarceration.

Further, youth in the adult system are subject to mentally harmful practices and have less mental health services available to them than in the juvenile system. Many juveniles are placed in isolation, which can severely exacerbate or even cause mental disorders that have the potential to affect them for the rest of their lives. Tragically, youth housed in adult jails are 36 times more likely to commit suicide than those in juvenile facilities.

The Ultimate Consequences: Moral and Financial

Youth sentenced as adults receive an adult criminal record, which restricts them from many employment and educational opportunities as well as financial aid. We know from numerous research reports that a lack of education and employment means higher chances of recidivism.

So, it makes sense that young people who go through the adult system are 34 percent more likely than those in the juvenile system to be re-arrested. Not only is this devastating for these young individuals, it also perpetuates a larger cycle of youth incarceration that is incredibly expensive to taxpayers as they must continue to foot the bill for recidivism.

Solutions: Keeping Kids out of the Adult System

There are notable success stories that suggest keeping kids out of the adult system can be extremely beneficial.

Since 2005, 29 states and Washington, D.C. have passed laws to make it more difficult to prosecute and sentence juveniles as adults, including raising the age required for adult prosecution and establishing alternatives to detention.

New York started implementing reforms in 2011, during a period of budget struggles and several investigations by the Justice Department into failing juvenile facilities. The new task force established a program to keep young offenders in local juvenile facilities as well as focus on their education, mental health and substance abuse issues. Since then, the number of detained youth has declined by 45 percent.

After Texas passed laws to keep kids in facilities closer to home as well as decrease prosecution for minor offenses by students in school (like disrupting class or possessing tobacco), they cut the number of children in adult court by 83 percent.

Takeaway

As juveniles continue to be tried and imprisoned as adults, we continue to see all of the repercussions. Not only are juveniles at extreme risk of sexual and other abuse, which is inarguably unacceptable, they also get denied counseling and educational services they desperately need.

Thus, the time they spend in these facilities can set them back educationally, mentally and emotionally. These setbacks are enhanced by the adult criminal record they receive, preventing them from important educational and employment opportunities in the future.

All of these consequences result in a disproportionate amount of youth in adult facilities ending up incarcerated again later in life, which derails their futures and bankrupts the system.

The cycle does not benefit anyone, and it is far past time to push for reform in all 50 states.

EVALUATING THE AUTHOR'S ARGUMENTS:

How does viewpoint author Caitlin Curley use the emotional compass of readers to make her points in favor of rehabilitation and treatment over imprisonment? She brings up incidents of sexual abuse against juvenile inmates and also expresses optimism that times are changing based on the actions taken by several states in recent years.

Incarcerating Minors Is Detrimental to Public Health

"Youth of color are more likely to be tried as adults than White youth, even when being charged with similar crimes."

Human Impact Partners

In the following viewpoint, Human Impact Partners argues that the incarceration of minors has negatively impacted public health. The authors claim that underprivileged youths of color have been unfairly targeted for jail sentences, especially those in adult prisons. They believe that favoring punishment over rehabilitation goes against research by developmental scientists and remains a detriment to society. The authors make strong claims that locking up the young ignores the environmental causes of criminality and that the solution is treatment rather than punishment. Human Impact Partners is an organization that promotes public health equity.

AS YOU READ, CONSIDER THE FOLLOWING QUESTIONS:
1. Should fourteen-year-olds be responsible for their own actions?
2. How much harder is it for youth living in poverty to remain law-abiding citizens?
3. Should kids from inner-city neighborhoods receive greater access to programs that rehabilitate?

"Juvenile InJustice: Charging Youth as Adults Is Ineffective, Biased, and Harmful," Human Impact Partners, February 2017. Reprinted by permission.

Are white teens punished differently than youth of color who commit the same crime?

In all 50 states, youth under age 18 can be tried in adult criminal court through various types of juvenile transfer laws. In California, youth as young as 14 can be tried as adults at the discretion of a juvenile court judge. When young people are transferred out of the juvenile system, they are more likely to be convicted and typically receive harsher sentences than youth who remain in juvenile court charged with similar crimes.

This practice undermines the purpose of the juvenile court system, pursues punishment rather than rehabilitation, and conflicts with what we know from developmental science. Furthermore, laws that allow youth to be tried as adults reflect and reinforce the racial inequities that characterize the justice system in United States.

In this report, we review the process that unfolds when a young person is tried as an adult in California and evaluate the health and equity impacts of charging youth as adults. Our findings indicate that:

The Justice System Is Biased Against Youth of Color

Youth of color are overrepresented at every stage of the juvenile court system. Rampant racial inequities are evident in the way youth of color are disciplined in school, policed and arrested, detained, sentenced, and incarcerated. These inequities persist even after controlling for variables like offense severity and prior criminal record. Research shows that youth of color receive harsher sentences than White youth charged with similar offenses.

Youth of color are more likely to be tried as adults than White youth, even when being charged with similar crimes. In California in 2015, 88% of juveniles tried as adults were youth of color.

> *"As a society … do we want young people to be left to a specific, certain fate in prison … or do we want a process of education, a process of healing, a process of insight to support them to understand how they got there, a process of growth? What do we want?"*
>
> —*Malachi, charged as an adult at age 15*

"Tough on Crime" Laws Criminalize Youth and Are Ineffective

Research shows that "tough on crime" policy shifts during the 1980s and 1990s have negatively impacted youth, families, and communities of color. These laws were fueled by high-profile criminal cases involving youth, sensationalized coverage of system-involved youth by the media, and crusading politicians who warned that juvenile "super-predators" posed a significant threat to public safety. The general sentiment—not based on research or data—across the political spectrum was that treatment approaches and rehabilitation attempts did not work.

However, time has shown that harshly punishing youth by trying them in the adult system has failed as an effective deterrent. Several large-scale studies have found higher recidivism rates among juveniles tried and sentenced in adult court than among youth charged with similar offenses in juvenile court.

The Adult Court System Ignores the Environmental Factors That Affect Adolescent Behavior

When someone is charged in adult court, they are either found guilty or innocent—and they receive a punishment if they are found guilty. By contrast, the juvenile court system (at least in theory) is meant to focus on reasons for the youth's behavior rather than just their guilt or innocence. A juvenile court judge is responsible for reviewing that youth's case with their family, community, and future development in mind.

The following environmental factors affect youth behavior and are more likely to be ignored in the adult court system:

- Community disinvestment affects youth development and behavior. In low-income communities and communities of color, there are clear indicators of disinvestment rooted in historical trends and contemporary policies—including poor quality housing, under-resourced schools, scarce and low-paying jobs, and omnipresent police. These policies and their consequences marginalize communities, and the lack of opportunity influences young peoples' physical health and outlook on life.

Growing up in these neighborhoods puts children at risk for behavior considered "deviant" and antisocial.

- Poverty creates stress. Poverty prevents families from providing material needs and often reduces parents' presence in their children's lives. This can lead youth to take on a parental role in the family. This role switching, known as parentification, can impact a young person's life outlook and sense of self. It can force them to make hard choices and even engage in compromising behaviors. Youth that grow up in affluent households are protected from having to make these hard choices—and from being criminalized for their behavior when they act out.

- Childhood traumas can have long-term effects. Research shows that there is a strong link between childhood trauma (for example physical or emotional abuse or witnessing violence in the community) and a variety of physical and mental health outcomes, including disruptive behavior, antisocial behavior, psychosis, and mood disorders. System-involved youth are likely to have lived through Adverse Childhood Experiences (ACEs).

- Youth do not make decisions like adults. It is common and normal for youth to engage in risky behaviors that may negatively impact their health. In fact, our brains reward us for these risky behaviors when we are adolescents. Research shows that this phenomenon has an important developmental function: these early risk-taking experiences prepare us for adulthood, leading us to be more willing to take on important new challenges later in life, such as starting a job or leaving home. Charging youth as adults directly ignores this science of adolescent development.

Incarceration Undermines Youth Health and Well-Being

When we lock up young people, they are more likely to be exposed to extreme violence, fall prey to abuse, and suffer from illness. High rates of violence, unchecked gang activity, and overcrowding persist in Division of Juvenile Justice facilities where many youth sentenced as adults start their incarceration. Fights frequently erupt in facility dayrooms and school areas.

Even if young people manage to escape direct physical abuse in juvenile or adult facilities, exposure and proximity to violence can be harmful in and of itself. Research suggests that exposure to violence can lead to issues with development in youth.

Families of Incarcerated Youth Experience Negative Impacts

Parents and family members of system-involved youth are systematically excluded from the adult court process—they are not given meaningful opportunities to help determine what happens to their children. The inability to participate fully while their loved one is going through the system can be mentally and emotionally harmful to families.

In addition, contact with the justice system often entails exorbitant expenses that can worsen family poverty. The economic burden of legal fees, court costs, restitution payments, and visitation expenses can have disastrous and long-lasting financial consequences for families.

Solutions Exist

- Eliminate the practice of charging youth as adults under any circumstance.
- Require that system professionals undergo additional hands-on training and coaching by formerly incarcerated people and local community organizations on topics such as youth development, community history, trauma, implicit bias, institutional and structural racism, and the structural causes of crime.
- Implement community-oriented and problem-oriented policing according to promising practices, with primary aims of improving community safety and reducing contact between youth and law enforcement.
- Implement school and community-based restorative and transformative justice approaches focused on healing as an alternative to the court system for most youth.

- Research and pilot viable alternatives to sentencing for youth who commit serious crimes.
- Ensure support for families as they navigate the justice system— especially investing in peer mentoring strategies that link families and formerly incarcerated people.
- Increase inter-agency collaboration.
- Increase funding for quality and culturally appropriate wrap-around services for youth and their families, including programs that connect youth to traditional practices of community building and healing.
- Change school funding and education policy to provide quality and culturally appropriate education in all communities and ensure equitable distribution of educational resources and opportunities.
- Implement justice reinvestment strategies and other forms of investment in low-income communities of color to expand opportunity for youth of color and their families.

EVALUATING THE AUTHORS' ARGUMENTS:

The viewpoint authors cite sentencing differences based on race and economic status and also make suggestions that promote change. How do the authors use unfairness as an argument against the juvenile justice system in the United States?

The Confinement of Juveniles with Adults May Be Unconstitutional

"Numerous factors contribute to why juveniles face significant dangers when confined with adults."

Andrea Wood

In the following excerpted viewpoint, Andrea Wood uses a wide range of statistical data to argue that minors are more likely than older prisoners to be mistreated in adult jails. Among the most emotionally, mentally, and physically dangerous is the sexual abuse that can prove permanently traumatic. It can also cause victims to become hardened criminals themselves and prevent them from ever embracing a healthy lifestyle even after their release. The author notes that juveniles often become violent as a way to mask their pain. Wood is an attorney who works at Equal Justice Works.

"Cruel and Unusual Punishment: Confining Juveniles with Adults After Graham and Miller," by Andrea Wood, Emory University School of Law, 2012. Reprinted by permission.

AS YOU READ, CONSIDER THE FOLLOWING QUESTIONS:
1. What are the worst realities minors in adult prisons face that prevent rehabilitation?
2. What statistics does the author offer that argue against youths being jailed alongside adults?
3. Why are suicide rates so much higher among youths in adult prisons as opposed to juvenile facilities?

J uveniles confined in jails and prisons face serious threats to their health and well-being. Juveniles in adult facilities face a high risk of physical and sexual abuse from guards and other inmates, and this abuse may have devastating and long-term consequences for the victimized juvenile. Juveniles confined in adult facilities also have dramatically higher rates of suicide than do their counterparts housed in juvenile facilities. While confined in adult facilities, juveniles lack access to services critical to their continued development and are particularly vulnerable to criminal socialization.

Juveniles face significantly higher rates of physical and sexual abuse in adult facilities than do adult inmates in the same facilities or juveniles housed in juvenile facilities. This abuse often begins immediately, within the first forty-eight hours of a juvenile's entry into an adult facility. Juveniles are five times more likely to be sexually assaulted in adult facilities than in juvenile facilities. Although juveniles made up only .2% of the prison population in 2005, they made up almost 1% of the substantiated incidents of inmate-on-inmate sexual violence in prisons that year. Juveniles constituted less than 1% of the jail population in 2005, but they made up 21% of all victims of substantiated incidents of inmate-on-inmate sexual violence in jails. In total, juveniles made up 7.7% of all victims of substantiated acts of sexual violence in prisons and jails carried out by other inmates, even though they made up less than 1% of the total detained and incarcerated population.

Sexual assault and rape may result in severe physical consequences, potentially exposing the victim to HIV/AIDS, hepatitis, and other sexually transmitted infections. Sexual activity between

Juveniles make up a disproportionate share of sexual abuse victims in the prison population.

men, which constitutes the vast majority of prison rape, accounts for more than 50% of all new HIV infections in the United States. Rates of HIV and confirmed AIDS are more than five times higher among those incarcerated in prisons than in the general population of the United States.

Sexual abuse has severe and long-term emotional and psychological consequences for juveniles that may last well into adulthood. Sexual abuse can lead to major depression and posttraumatic stress disorder. Juveniles who have been sexually abused may face problems with anger, impulse control, flashbacks, dissociative episodes, hopelessness, despair, and persistent distrust and withdrawal. Sexual abuse can increase tendencies toward criminal behavior and substance abuse in juveniles. Upon release from prison, victims of prison rape are more likely to become homeless or require government assistance due to the physical and psychological impacts of rape than are those who were not raped in prison.

Congress recognized the significant risks that juveniles face in adult facilities when it passed the Prison Rape Elimination Act of 2003 (PREA). PREA, which unanimously passed in the House of Representatives and Senate and was immediately enacted into law by President George W. Bush, sought to draw attention to and address the issues of rape and sexual victimization of individuals in custody.

The findings section of PREA highlights the increased risk of rape that juveniles face: "Young first-time offenders are at increased risk of sexual victimization. Juveniles are 5 times more likely to be sexually assaulted in adult rather than juvenile facilities—often within the first 48 hours of incarceration." PREA requires prison officials to keep more thorough internal records on rape, and it created a commission to propose standards to improve prison management. Although an important symbolic step, PREA has failed to eliminate or reduce sexual abuse in correctional facilities or to demonstrably change public attitudes toward rape in custodial settings.

Numerous factors contribute to why juveniles face significant dangers when confined with adults. In a Department of Justice report that described characteristics that make an individual more likely to be sexually abused while incarcerated, many of the listed characteristics are common in juveniles, including small size and inexperience with the criminal justice system. Additionally, juveniles, who have not fully matured physically, cognitively, socially, or emotionally, are less capable of protecting themselves from sexual advances and assault. These juveniles generally also lack the experiences to cope in predatory environments, and expressions of fear may be taken as indications of weakness.

Staffing differences may also contribute to the high rates of sexual abuse in adult detention and correctional facilities because juvenile facilities generally have a much higher staff-to-inmate ratio than do adult facilities. Juvenile detention facilities generally have a ratio of one staff member to every eight youths, while an average adult jail has a staff-to-inmate ratio of one to sixty-four. The additional staff members in juvenile facilities may provide increased supervision and may also offer assistance and support to juveniles in a more focused manner.

Incidents of sexual assault in jails and prisons are underreported, and juveniles may be particularly discouraged from reporting sexual abuse as a result of developmental, emotional, and systemic barriers. The ramifications of disclosure include shame, stigma, not being believed, and retaliation, which impact juveniles more significantly than adults. Juveniles may not be willing to undergo the intense scrutiny needed to determine the accuracy of a report of sexual assault.

Once faced with formal interviews and investigation, juveniles may feel intimidated by the perpetrator, try to suppress the pain stemming from the abuse by denying it ever occurred, change their story, or refuse to cooperate with investigators.

Juveniles incarcerated in adult facilities are also at a high risk of committing suicide. One study indicates that a juvenile housed in an adult jail is five times more likely to commit suicide than is a juvenile in the general population and eight times more likely to commit suicide than is a juvenile housed in a juvenile facility. Other studies suggest that a juvenile's increased risk of suicide in adult jails may be far higher.

Not designed to meet the special needs of juveniles, adult facilities may seriously compromise a juvenile's healthy development, and surveys of adult facilities indicate that they generally lack specialized or developmentally appropriate programming for juveniles. Adult facilities are generally far less equipped than juvenile facilities to meet the educational needs of juveniles. In 95% of juvenile facilities, one teacher is employed for every fifteen inmates, in contrast to one teacher for every one hundred inmates in adult facilities. Unlike in adult facilities, the educational staff members in juvenile facilities are generally full-time employees. In addition to an overall higher staff-to-inmate ratio and more teachers, most juvenile facilities also include classroom spaces and do not have the same physical-space restrictions faced by many adult facilities. Juveniles confined in adult facilities, especially those in pretrial detention awaiting adjudication, face a high risk of falling more behind in their education.

Juvenile facilities are better able to provide developmentally appropriate healthcare, rehabilitative services, and programming than are adult facilities. Adult facilities may fail to provide juveniles with the appropriate nutrition or dental and vision care, which are especially critical for developing adolescents. Staff members at juvenile facilities typically receive special training to work with juveniles not generally received by the staff at adult facilities. Many adult facilities fail to provide juveniles with even basic services, including prison-survival skills and counseling. In two-thirds of juvenile facilities, one counselor is employed for every ten juveniles, and in 85% of juvenile facilities, at least one counselor is employed for every twenty-five juveniles. A direct comparison to the number of counselors available in adult facilities is difficult because most adult facilities group all "professional and technical" personnel in one category, which includes all medical and classification staff. This staff-to-inmate ratio is one to twenty-five. Given their incomplete development, juveniles are significantly impacted by the lack of appropriate services and care in adult facilities.

Juveniles' developmental stage and malleability make them particularly vulnerable to criminal socialization when incarcerated with adults. Generally sensitive to peer pressure as a group, juveniles confined in adult facilities are "especially likely to engage in violent behavior and to develop identities linked to domination and control." While confined in adult facilities, juveniles lack models for building a positive identity, honing productive life skills, and solving problems and disputes. Rather, juveniles may spend considerable amounts of time with experienced adult offenders, who may pass along new methods and techniques related to criminal activity and the avoidance of detection.

Juveniles may also adopt violent practices to mask their vulnerable status. To survive the violence they encounter in adult facilities, juveniles have reported that they often attempt to fit in to inmate culture. Many juveniles can only adjust to life in adult prisons or jails by "accepting violence as a part of daily life and, thus, becoming even more violent."

A body of evidence suggests that incarcerating juveniles in adult correctional facilities not only places the juveniles in a demonstrably more hazardous living situation but also does not fulfill commonly accepted purposes of punishment. Research indicates that incarcerating juveniles with adults, an often more experienced criminal population, may neither deter juveniles from future criminal activity nor improve public safety. In 2007, the Task Force on Community Preventive Services, supported by the Centers for Disease Control and Prevention, systematically evaluated published studies that dealt with the effectiveness of policies that result in the transfer of juveniles to criminal court. The task force scrutinized the design suitability, methodologies, execution, and outcomes of these studies.

In its analysis of six studies examining specific deterrence, all of which controlled for selection bias, the task force noted that four studies found that transferred juveniles subsequently committed more violent and cumulative crime than their counterparts who remained in the juvenile justice system. These four studies indicate that transferred juveniles were 33.7% more likely to be re-arrested than juveniles who remained in the juvenile justice system. The task force concluded that "juveniles transferred to the adult justice system have greater rates of subsequent violence than juveniles retained in the juvenile justice system" and that "[t]ransferring juveniles to the adult justice system is counterproductive as a strategy for deterring subsequent violence." This increase in recidivism may be partially attributable to confinement in adult facilities, given that juveniles are held with more experienced adult offenders and lack the rehabilitative opportunities available in juvenile facilities. Some researchers have concluded that incarceration with adults may have "brutalizing effects" on juveniles, in which the violent experiences that juveniles witness and experience in adult facilities normalize violent and criminal conduct.

Research is generally inconclusive as to whether conviction in criminal court and incarceration in adult facilities deters potential juvenile offenders. Most evidence indicates that transfer to criminal court and incarceration in adult facilities has little or no general deterrent effect. Accordingly, an accumulating body of evidence suggests that incarcerating juveniles in adult facilities fails to demonstrably deter future crime, and perhaps even increases recidivism rates in juvenile offenders, while dramatically increasing the risk of serious harm faced by these vulnerable wards of the state.

Although some seek to justify the confinement of juveniles with adults by pointing to the need for increased criminal sanctions for certain hardened juvenile offenders, many juveniles who are convicted of criminal offenses and confined in adult facilities serve sentences comparable in length to the ones that they would have served if held in juvenile facilities. Seventy-eight percent of juveniles incarcerated in adult facilities are released before they turn twenty-one; ninety-five percent are released before they turn twenty-five. The average time that these juveniles serve on their sentences is two years and eight months. Additionally, some jurisdictions have implemented systems in which a juvenile convicted in criminal court can serve his sentence in a juvenile detention facility until he reaches the age of eighteen, at which time he can be transferred to an adult facility to serve the remaining time of his sentence if necessary.

Juveniles housed in adult facilities face extreme risks to their health and well-being without the benefit of developmentally appropriate services and rehabilitative programming. Exposed to alarmingly high rates of physical and sexual abuse, these children face the real possibility of developing psychological and emotional disorders, contracting sexually transmitted infections, or even committing suicide. Adult facilities, with often dramatically lower staff-to-inmate ratios than juvenile facilities, are not equipped to handle the special educational, developmental, physical, and emotional needs of juveniles, and thus deprive them of critical opportunities for rehabilitation. In fact, confinement in adult facilities may foster more violent behaviors, facilitate opportunities for criminal socialization, and increase recidivism.

EVALUATING THE AUTHOR'S ARGUMENTS:

Viewpoint author Andrea Wood cites a wide range of statistics to support her argument. Does she cover the entirety of the issues revolving around the sexual abuse of juveniles in adult prisons?

Juvenile Detention Enables Criminals

"A profit-based model of incarceration will measure success in profit. Only a therapeutic model will judge itself on therapeutic outcomes."

Shauneen Lambe

In the following viewpoint, Shauneen Lambe argues that juvenile detention has the opposite effect of its intent. The author contends that her visits to jails in the United States and Britain left her disgusted over their treatment of minors. She rails against a high level of violence experienced by imprisoned youths in supposedly civilized nations, but she expresses optimism that the decreasing number of youths in adult prisons shows that times are changing for the better. Lambe is an attorney and joint chief executive of Just for Kids Law.

AS YOU READ, CONSIDER THE FOLLOWING QUESTIONS:

1. Should jails operate for profit, according to the author?
2. Does the prison system focus not enough on rehabilitation and too much on punishment?
3. How does the author compare the prison systems in Britain and America?

Does juvenile incarceration breed a generation of future prisoners?

In 2003 I visited Feltham young offender institution for the first time. Freshly returned from death row in America, I was feeling smug about civilised Britain. I walked down a concrete corridor with no walls—just bars—the wind whipping through a derelict garden with a small pond where a plastic heron lay prone, beak down in the sludge. Then, an enormous, brightly lit visitors' room with tables nailed to the floor, and in the corner a holding cell, three sides of which were glass, holding at least 10 children. None of them were talking.

I had never been in an environment so eerily quiet. Anyone who has spent any time in schools knows that kids are noisy. Yet here were 10 teenagers sitting together, and none of them had anything to say.

In my years working as a lawyer visiting Feltham, I heard many distressing stories. There was the child who, when he was first incarcerated, was sick all night, with no adult coming to help him clear it up or see if he was OK. There was the child who witnessed guards unlocking the cells to enable a gang to attack another child in the shower. I heard of professionals visiting the medical wing to see severely disturbed children, sometimes naked, being held in glass cells. One teenager—who had nine GCSEs—told me that the only education they received was a wordsearch.

So I wasn't surprised when Panorama revealed last year that there were high levels of violence and use of force at the G4S-run Medway secure training centre, a detention centre for younger and more vulnerable teenagers than are held at Feltham. Nor was I surprised when, in July 2017, the chief inspector of prisons said that youth custody

FAST FACT

The number of children in England and Wales sentenced to custody from 2007 to 2017 fell about 74 percent.

centres in England and Wales were so unsafe that a "tragedy" was "inevitable," and that "not a single establishment inspected was safe to hold young people."

I was, however, surprised to hear Cressida Dick, the Metropolitan police commissioner, say in a speech at the AGM of prison reform charity the Howard League this month that teenage law-breakers should face "harsher and more effective" prison sentences that were a "real deterrent to criminals."

Not only is this false, it also shows Dick to be ignorant of the extensive academic evidence. Prison, as it exists in the UK and other western countries including the US, has never been effective in preventing future crimes. In fact my experience suggests the opposite. I believe that in this country youth prisons are the perfect environment for children to fall further into criminality, whether it is by failing to educate them, teaching them to protect themselves from violence, enabling them to develop gang relationships, or failing to provide support upon their release.

I can confidently say that most of the young people I have worked with, over nearly 15 years, had a harder time breaking the cycle of crime after a spell in custody than those who remained in the community. The latter were reintegrated by having their needs addressed, be they mental health problems or issues with education, peer groups or immigration status.

If the institutions that Dick was suggesting we send children to had successful education programmes, staff who were trained and qualified to work with young people, therapeutic support and reintegration programmes, there might be some debate to be had about the length of sentences. There are places where these type of institutions exist, such as Spain, which has the Diagrama re-education centre (which would like to move into the UK); or Norway, where there are therapeutic units. Both models state that their role is to help return children to the community in a better position than when they came in.

But these models are expensive and we are in a time of austerity. It is impossible to envisage this government committing the resources required to ensure that troubled and complex adolescents get the support they require.

The number of children incarcerated in the UK has gone down, from 3,000 in 2007 to around 860 today. And that is a good thing. If there is anything we can learn from the Panorama documentary, it is that the cost to the taxpayer of a bed at Medway far exceeds the cost of a bed at Feltham; and while that was undoubtedly good for the shareholders at G4S, it was not for the children held there. A profit-based model of incarceration will measure success in profit. Only a therapeutic model will judge itself on therapeutic outcomes.

Carolyne Willow, the director of the charity Article 39, recently wrote a book called *Children Behind Bars*. When we met, she told me one thing that, among the stories of sanctioned violence, regular strippings and deprivation of human contact, has stayed with me. It was that a parent is never allowed to see the space that their incarcerated child has been living and sleeping in, unless their child dies. Any therapist in the world will tell you that positive family relationships lead to better lives. Yet only after a death in custody is a parent given access to their child's day-to-day environment.

The state-enforced removal of a child has never sounded more cruel. In William Shakespeare's *Richard III*, when her children were locked in the Tower of London, Queen Elizabeth, wife of King Edward IV, said: "Pity, you ancient stones, those tender babes / Whom envy hath immur'd within your walls – / Rough cradle for such little pretty ones."

Over 500 years of social progress have passed, and yet when it comes to locking up children, it seems we are still in the same place.

EVALUATING THE AUTHOR'S ARGUMENTS:

How does viewpoint author Shauneen Lambe compare the British system of juvenile justice to that of the United States? Is the comparison a successful way to convey the author's opinions about juvenile justice?

Instead of Locking Up Kids, Teach Them to Care for Their Community

"Community work is harder than locking kids up—it takes more creativity, more dedication."

Shaena Fazal

In the following viewpoint, Shaena Fazal argues that policy makers and communities must take a far more creative and productive approach to the problem of youth criminality. The author suggests that community service provides minors with a sense of value and self-pride in hard work and allows them to gain an appreciation of positively contributing to society. Fazal understands that treating all children the same and simply locking them up for particular crimes does not take into consideration their individual needs and circumstances while stifling self-expression and weakening self-image. Fazal is national policy director for Youth Advocate Programs.

"A Much-Needed Alternative to Youth Prisons," by Shaena Fazal, Esq. Chief of Public Policy, Advocacy and External Communications, July 15, 2015. Reprinted by permission.

1. How is rehabilitating youthful offenders an investment in the future of America?
2. Is enough being done to study and fix the root causes of juvenile crime?
3. Should communities be given more responsibility for rehabilitating minor lawbreakers?

In June, Patrick McCarthy, the president of the Annie E. Casey Foundation delivered a TED Talk in which he advocated for closing youth prisons, stating: "I believe it's long past time to close these inhumane, ineffective, wasteful factories of failure once and for all. Every one of them. We need to admit that what we're doing doesn't work, and is making the problem worse while costing billions of dollars and ruining thousands of lives."

We couldn't agree more.

If we don't incarcerate young people in conflict with the law, what do we do with them?

The answer is simple: We care for and invest in our young people; resource families and communities to safely hold youth accountable; invest in each young person's success, and; address the root causes of youth crime in the communities where the youth live, all in the context of their homes and neighborhoods.

Many juvenile justice administrators agree community-based programs are the right approach for young people in the justice system, but still maintain spending ratios that favor institutions over families and communities. According to the Justice Policy Institute, this institutional bias costs hundreds of thousands of dollars a day per youth, or $5 billion a year. Every year, taxpayers spend between eight and 21 billion dollars on indirect costs of youth incarceration, like future lost wages, lost educational opportunities and reliance on public assistance. Several states spend significant portions of their budgets sending young people to private residential treatment centers, often with poor long-term results.

Systems that redirect the dollars they currently spend on confinement into communities that send the most young people to

Community programs such as Boys & Girls Clubs can steer kids in the right direction.

detention, state prison or other confinement, have a better chance of achieving public safety, positive youth outcomes and racial equity.

That's because public safety is about much more than prisons and police. It's about all the things that characterize safe neighborhoods—access to good schools and jobs, and opportunities to learn, grow, develop and play in safe environments.

The evidence is clear that what works to achieve positive outcomes for any young person, also works for young people in the juvenile justice system: recognizing the individuality of each youth; including their families; building on their strengths; keeping them safe; knowing who connects best with them; helping them navigate difficult situations in their lives; finding opportunities for them to thrive, grow and develop, and; ensuring access to quality education and meaningful opportunities to work.

This country's institutional bias is at the heart of racial inequity in the juvenile justice system. Many communities that send the most young people to detention or prison are black and brown neighborhoods drained of resources designed to engage and help justice involved youth. Responding to this lack of resources with youth incarceration is the easy, but wrong, thing to do. These communities should be saturated with effective, culturally competent programs and resources to engage neighbors in helping their youth.

Every community and juvenile justice system in this country knows which neighborhoods and even blocks send the most kids to detention and youth prisons. That is where the redirected dollars should go to develop robust, comprehensive continuums of care that include an array of services, supports and creative interventions for young people who need them.

A comprehensive continuum of care for justice involved youth is more than stringing together a few types of alternative programs for some kids

while hundreds of young people continue on to youth prison or residential placements far from their communities. Instead, a comprehensive system takes a holistic approach to youth in need before they get to the justice system and after they're there, addressing the root causes of behavior that can lead to delinquency or even youth crime. A comprehensive continuum will:

- Ensure that kids who do not need to be in the juvenile justice system stay out of the system
- Maintain enough services to serve almost all justice involved youth and their families in their homes, especially youth with the most complex needs. For young people with complex needs, programs should include the elements listed in our recent report, "Safely Home."
- Intentionally focus on reducing racial and ethnic disparity in policy and practice
- Hold youth accountable for their behavior without resorting to incarceration
- Help youth access opportunities to give back so they can be contributors to their community, not just receivers of service, resulting in a restored sense of belonging
- Focus interventions on the youth and his or her family and peers
- Individualize services to meet the needs and build on the strengths of each unique young person
- Ensure that services and supports will be available 24/7 at times when young people and their families need help the most

- Arrange for access to job or vocational training, education and meaningful work
- Create opportunities for young people to learn new skills and responses to negative stimuli and practice them in their community
- Support youth to meet their obligations to pay restitution
- Connect young people to credible messengers—caring adults who live in a youth's community, understand the neighborhood and a youth's culture. Credible messengers are trained in youth development and establish a trusting relationship with the youth and family.

With the right investment and supports, continuums of care will enhance, not compromise public safety. An effective continuum of care works at the front end, so that youth who would ordinarily be sent to youth prison can stay safely at home with their families. It also works at the back end to bring young people currently confined in youth prisons safely home to their families and neighborhoods.

One community that created a continuum is Toledo, Ohio's Lucas County Juvenile Court, led by Judge Denise Navarre Cubbon and Juvenile Court Administrator Deborah Hodges. As we highlighted in the report "Safely Home," in 1998, Lucas County sent over 300 young people to the state's youth prisons. Last year, that number was down to 17. In a recent conversation with Ms. Hodges, we learned that number dropped even more—in the last fiscal year, Lucas County sent 10 young people to state prison.

They also led significant reductions in the county's detention population. From 2009 to the first quarter of 2014 the average daily population decreased by 72%. During this same time period, the average daily population for black youth in the Juvenile Detention Center also decreased by 71%.

To achieve these reductions, Lucas County essentially shifted from a facility-based juvenile justice system in 1998 to a community-based juvenile justice system. At the front end, Lucas County created an Assessment Center to make sure that young people who did not need to be in the system stayed out. Each youth presented to the Center is screened for an appropriate response. Lucas County also built enough services in the community so that the detention center or the state prisons were not the only places for young people to get services they needed. For kids with complex needs, they partnered with our organization, Youth Advocate Programs, to provide intensive mentoring and wraparound programs that work with youth, their families and their communities.

And rather than sending young people away to prison when the services they need did not exist, Lucas County created new services, such as a program to address the high numbers of young people—and especially kids of color—entering their courtrooms through school-based charges. The state reform efforts, Reclaim Ohio and Targeted Reclaim, which focuses on redirecting resources from facilities to community, also played a role in supporting alternatives and reducing Lucas County's juvenile population. The dollars they saved in using confinement less, enabled the County to build a strong continuum of care for juveniles in their own community.

Community work is harder than locking kids up—it takes more creativity, more dedication and requires moving beyond a "one-size-fits-all" approach. But it is what our young people and their families need to thrive, and what our communities need to be safe. Many of the youth in our care have been affected by extreme poverty, discrimination, disability, trauma and abuse, lack of early guidance and opportunity, poor schools and availability of guns and drugs. They are survivors who need support and access to their families and positive opportunities, not removal and isolation.

Yes, close youth prisons. And let's invest in our young people and their communities. Because when communities are properly resourced, anything that can be done in a youth prison can be done in the community, only better.

EVALUATING THE AUTHOR'S ARGUMENTS:

How does viewpoint author Shaena Fazal use the example of one county in Ohio to promote rehabilitation over imprisonment for youths? Is this an effective way to support her argument?

Chapter 3

Does Age Matter?

Does locking up juvenile offenders work in the long run? What is best for society overall?

Viewpoint

1

Children Should Not Be Sentenced to Life Behind Bars

Gretchen Gavett and Sarah Childress

In the following viewpoint, Gretchen Gavett and Sarah Childress examine a 2012 Supreme Court decision that ruled unconstitutional the life sentencing without parole of youths under age eighteen. The authors cite several individual cases of youth offenders who were positively affected by the ruling. The Supreme Court decision, which was applauded by youth advocates, was considered a step in the right direction in a country coming to grips with the futility of locking up its minors. Gavett is a former producer for digital media for *FRONTLINE*. Childress is a senior reporter for *FRONTLINE*.

"The US is one of the few countries in the world that allows children under 18 to be prosecuted as adults and sentenced to life without parole."

AS YOU READ, CONSIDER THE FOLLOWING QUESTIONS:

1. Which amendment did the Supreme Court find is violated by mandatory life sentences without parole for minors?
2. Why is Jacob Ind serving a life sentence?
3. Is the possibility of parole enough of a motivation for jailed minors to rehabilitate?

"Supreme Court Bans Mandatory Life Terms for Kids: What It Means," by Gretchen Gavett and Sarah Childress, from *FRONTLINE*, "Second Chance Kids" (https://www.pbs.org/wgbh/frontline/article/supreme-court-bans-mandatory-lifeterms-for-kids-what-it-means/) ©1995-2018 WGBH Educational Foundation.

In a close decision, the US Supreme Court introduced the possibility of parole for juveniles sentenced to life in prison.

This morning, the United States Supreme Court ruled 5–4 that the mandatory sentencing of a juvenile under the age of 18 to life in prison without the possibility of parole is unconstitutional.

The majority opinion, written by Justice Elena Kagan, said that the policy violates the Eighth Amendment, which prohibits cruel and unusual punishment. Kagan argued that previous case law shows that children lack the maturity to make sound decisions, and that mandatory sentencing leaves no room for discretion. "… [I]mposition of a State's most severe penalties on juvenile offenders cannot proceed as though they were not children," she wrote.

The decision would still allow a judge to use discretion to assign a life sentence without parole to juveniles. But Kagan said that would be rare: "Given all we have said in *Roper, Graham* [previous rulings that banned the life sentence without parole in non-homicide cases, and the death penalty for juveniles] and this decision about children's diminished culpability and heightened capacity for change, we think appropriate occasions for sentencing juveniles to this harshest possible penalty will be uncommon."

"It really is a historic ruling, but in our opinion it doesn't go far enough," because it stopped short from banning the policy outright, said Alison Parker, the director of Human Rights Watch's US program. But, she added: "It does bring the US more in line with the rest of the world."

The US is one of the few countries in the world that allows children under 18 to be prosecuted as adults and sentenced to life without parole; 29 states have such laws on the books, according to the ACLU. There are more than 2,500 people currently in jail nationwide who fall under this category; 79 of them were sentenced when they were 14 or younger. About 70 percent of the latter category are black or Latino.

Today's decision follows two recent rulings that limited the type of penalties that can be doled out to underage defendants. In 2005, the Supreme Court ruled that sentencing juveniles to death was unconstitutional; four years later, the court decided the same for juveniles sentenced to life without the possibility of parole in cases that did not involve a homicide.

With today's ruling, people who were sentenced to life without parole as juveniles will be entitled to new sentencing hearings in which judges will consider their character, life circumstances and age in determining an appropriate sentence, said Bryan Stevenson, executive director of the Equal Justice Initiative, in a statement. Stevenson represents both Kuntrell Jackson and Evan Miller, the two young men named in the cases ruled on by the court.

"This is an important win for children," Stevenson said. "The court has recognized that children need additional attention and protection in the criminal justice system."

Here is more on the two cases that the court ruled on today, as well as the cases of two individuals featured in our 2007 film *When Kids Get Life*.

Kuntrell Jackson

The 14 year old was living in Arkansas when he took part in a video store robbery with two other boys that ended in the shooting death of 28-year-old clerk, Laurie Troop.

Jackson, however, wasn't the triggerman. Another boy, Derrick Shields, shot Troop with a sawed-off shotgun after she said she didn't have any money.

At his trial, Jackson's lawyer argued that he was outside the store acting as the lookout, when the murder took place. Prosecutors said he was closer to the crime, claiming that Jackson told Troop, "We ain't playin'" before Shields shot her. But his defense team argued that Jackson said, "I thought you all was playin'," indicating he was unaware of his co-conspirator's violent intentions.

Because Arkansas has a felony murder statute, Jackson, who was tried as an adult, was deemed just as responsible as Shields in the murder because it took place during the process of another felony: the robbery. Jackson was convicted and sentenced to life in prison without the possibility of parole.

His crime took place in 1999; he is now 26. Following today's ruling, his attorney says he's entitled to a new sentencing hearing.

Evan Miller

On July 15, 2003, 14-year-old Miller and a friend, Colby Smith, went to the trailer home of a neighbor, Cole Cannon looking for drugs.

Cannon was passed out from drinking and doing drugs, so Miller stole $300 from Cannon's wallet, as well as his driver's license. But as he put back the wallet, Cannon woke up and attacked him. Miller and Smith started beating him with fists and a bat. When Cannon was still, they covered him with a sheet. To hide the evidence, they set the trailer on fire. Cannon, who was still alive, burned to death.

Miller initially denied any involvement in the crime, but later admitted to stealing the money and the license. His attorneys, asking for leniency, argued that Miller had been the victim of domestic abuse throughout his childhood. Miller was convicted of capital murder and given the mandatory sentence of life without the possibility of parole.

Now in his early 20s, Miller is also entitled to a new sentencing hearing following today's ruling.

Jacob Ind

In 1992, when he was 15, Jacob Ind hired a classmate to kill his mother and stepfather after what he says were years of physical, emotional and sexual abuse. When the classmate botched the job, Ind, awakened by the gunshots and the ensuing struggle, fired the fatal shots using his stepfather's .357 Magnum revolver.

After the killings, Ind seemed detached from the reality of what he'd done. "I didn't really grasp the permanency of their deaths," he told *FRONTLINE*. "I definitely didn't understand the gravity of what it means to kill somebody."

"I remember I was sitting in the police station—and this is how out of touch of reality I was," he continued. "I had a small amount of marijuana, like an eighth of an ounce, in my bedroom. And I'm telling my brother, 'You got to get the marijuana or else I'm in trouble.' I'm arrested for first-degree murder, and I don't think I'm in trouble!"

Ind was tried as an adult and, despite his brother's testimony about their stepfather's abuse, was convicted of two counts of first-degree murder on June 17, 1994. As a juvenile, he was not eligible for the death penalty; instead, he was given a mandatory sentence of life without parole. As of 2007, more than half of his time in prison was spent in the state supermax, Colorado State Penitentiary, where he spent 23 hours a day in solitary confinement. He was sent there in 1995 when contraband was found in his cell.

Jacob Ind is now in his mid-30s. His attorney could not be immediately reached for comment.

Andrew Medina

At 15, Medina was living on the streets, using drugs and paling around with two other kids, Michael Brown and Derrick Miller. The three cooked up a carjacking scheme to make some money.

On July 15, 1999, Kristopher Lohrmeyer, 17, was preparing to drive home after his shift at the Colorado City Creamery, an ice-cream shop. Brown distracted him, and then Medina and Miller demanded his keys and cash. Someone fired a shot through the car's back window, killing Lohrmeyer.

Brown and Miller cut deals with the prosecution, and said Medina was the shooter. He alone faced the first-degree murder charge, and a mandatory sentence of life without parole. He's currently serving time in the Colorado State Penitentiary, a high-security prison.

Medina told Human Rights Watch in 2004 that he had reformed his life since his time in prison: "[I was a different] person—just the way I talk and the way I am—the way I carry myself. I don't know, maybe it's just what I've experienced. I know a lot of people, they say you have to do things to change, but I don't think that's true. I think a person's change … just happens. And it's happened to me."

One of Medina's lawyers, Darren Cantor, said that it wasn't yet clear how the Supreme Court ruling would affect his client, but that he's almost certainly entitled to a re-sentencing hearing. "There never should have been life without parole for juveniles," he told *FRONTLINE* on Monday. "It's insane."

EVALUATING THE AUTHORS' ARGUMENTS:

Did the viewpoint authors take the correct track by citing several individual cases to support the Supreme Court ruling that banned life sentences without the possibility of parole? Could they have made their case by presenting examples from both sides of the argument?

Raise the Age, Reduce Recidivism

Teresa Wiltz

"Young brains aren't fully developed until around age 25 and youth don't fully understand the consequences of their actions."

In the following viewpoint, Teresa Wiltz argues that raising the age at which a juvenile can be jailed would result in a positive step for the well-being of youth and for society overall. The author further states that prisons are used only for punishment and have never been proved a deterrent to crime for kids, many of whom don't fully grasp the significance of their actions and the impact they have on themselves and others. Wiltz is a veteran journalist who covers welfare, housing, and social services for Stateline.

AS YOU READ, CONSIDER THE FOLLOWING QUESTIONS:

1. Is it fair that those too young to vote can be tried and imprisoned as adults?
2. Should only adults twenty-one and older be sent to adult prisons?
3. Are crimes such as murder enough to justify young teenage imprisonment?

"How 'Raise the Age' Laws Might Reduce Recidivism," by Teresa Wiltz, The Pew Charitable Trusts, May 31, 2017. Reprinted by permission.

Minors aren't considered mature enough to vote or drink alcohol. Is it fair to punish them as adults?

You have to be 18 to vote in a general election or join the military without your parents' consent—and you've got to be 21 before you can belly up to the bar.

But in some states, if you're under 18 and you break the law, you'll be treated as an adult, no matter how slight the crime—even if it's just jumping a subway turnstile or shoplifting.

Sixteen-year-olds in New York and North Carolina are still funneled through adult criminal courts and housed in adult prisons and jails. In Georgia, Michigan, Missouri, Texas and Wisconsin, 17-year-olds are automatically prosecuted as adults.

Raising the age can have a huge impact on the lives of young people. Teens funneled into adult prisons do not have access to rehabilitative services that the juvenile justice system provides. And adult prisons can be extremely dangerous for teens.

Prosecuting minors as adults used to be more common. But the practice has declined amid increasing awareness that young people, with brains that are still developing, may not fully understand the consequences of their actions, as well as evidence that teens are more likely to commit additional crimes if they are prosecuted as adults.

Over the past decade, at least seven states have raised the age of criminal responsibility to 18, and today most states set it there. And more changes are on the way.

In New York, under a law signed by Democratic Gov. Andrew Cuomo in April, 16-year-olds charged with a crime will no longer automatically be prosecuted as an adult after October 2018. A year later, 17-year-olds will no longer automatically be prosecuted as an adult, with that decision left to a judge in felony cases.

And this month, after years of debate, the North Carolina House overwhelmingly passed a bill that would raise the age of criminal responsibility to 18.

North Carolina state Rep. Duane Hall, a former public defender who sponsored the legislation there, said he's seen how a permanent adult conviction can destroy a young life. "A kid who gets into a fight at a football game in North Carolina could have an adult conviction," the Democrat said.

Meanwhile, lawmakers in Georgia, Michigan and Missouri are considering legislation that would raise the age of criminal responsibility from 17 to 18. (A similar bill failed to make it to a vote in Wisconsin last year because of concerns over cost.) Since 2007, Connecticut, Illinois, Louisiana, Massachusetts, Mississippi, New Hampshire and South Carolina have all enacted laws raising the age to 18.

Some states are taking things a step further: In February, Connecticut Gov. Dannel Malloy, a Democrat, introduced a bill that would make the state one of the first to raise the age of criminal responsibility to 21. And last year, Vermont enacted a law that will gradually raise the age of criminal responsibility from 18 to 21 by July 2018 and create a separate prison for incarcerated youth up to age 25.

The goal is to steer older teens into the juvenile court system, where they can participate in counseling and diversion programs such as substance abuse treatment and educational assistance.

"There's a general understanding that teenagers and young adults make bad decisions that shouldn't prevent them from living their

FAST FACT

Many believe it is unfair that juveniles under 18 can be tried and prosecuted as adults but cannot vote until they turn 18 and cannot drink alcohol until they are 21.

lives going forward," said Nancy Ginsburg, director of adolescent intervention and diversion for the New York–based Legal Aid Society, a nonprofit advocacy group that helped craft the New York legislation.

By charging and convicting adolescents as adults, Ginsburg said, "you basically create a whole class of people who cannot be employed and cannot obtain housing for no other reason than we decided to hold them accountable for things that they did when they were young."

There are several reasons behind the nationwide push to raise the age. One is the growing awareness that young brains aren't fully developed until around age 25 and youth don't fully understand the consequences of their actions.

Advocates also point to evidence that teens who've been arrested are less likely to commit additional crimes if they are prosecuted as minors, and to the fact that young people incarcerated in adult prisons are at a much greater risk of sexual assault than adult offenders.

Funneling more teens to juvenile courts initially may increase costs for state and local governments. But evidence suggests that prosecuting more youthful offenders in juvenile justice courts will save taxpayers money as recidivism rates are reduced and more youth are able to lead successful lives, earn a living, and contributing to the local economy.

But some critics, such as the Brooklyn NAACP, argue the New York law doesn't go far enough to protect children. Others, such as Bill Fitzpatrick, the district attorney for Onondaga County in upstate New York, argue the measures go too far.

"What are we going to do, raise the age to 26?" said Fitzpatrick, who serves as chairman of the National District Attorneys' Association. "The overwhelming majority of [prosecutors] recognize there's a difference between a 16-year-old and a 36-year-old, and we attempt to deal with them appropriately."

Relatively few young offenders are incarcerated in adult facilities, Fitzpatrick pointed out. In 2015, state prisons held an estimated 1,000 prisoners 17 or younger; federal prisons in April held 21 prisoners under 18 and 2,204 inmates 18 to 21 years old. Meanwhile, in 2015, fewer than 4,000 juveniles were in local jails.

"There's so much misinformation out there about juveniles being locked up and treated inappropriately," Fitzpatrick said.

Rehabilitation, Not Incarceration

Elizabeth Clarke, executive director of the Juvenile Justice Initiative, an advocacy group based in Evanston, Illinois, that pushed to raise the state's age of criminal responsibility to 18, said young people do better in the juvenile justice system, where the focus is on individual rehabilitation.

"There's no good that comes for kids out of adult court," Clarke said. "It's not a deterrent. This is really about what works and what's been shown to work."

Under the adult system, police were limited to two options: Arrest a suspect and send them to court or don't arrest and send them home. But the Illinois law meant greater leeway for handling 17-year-olds. Because they now are automatically treated as juveniles, police can send them to counseling, make them do community service, or simply make them write a letter of apology.

As a result of the law and other programs focused on rehabilitating troubled teens, the number of youth in the juvenile prison population has dropped from 1,195 to under 400 today, according to a Juvenile Justice Initiative analysis of Illinois Department of Juvenile Justice data. Three of the state's eight juvenile prisons have closed, and the number of youth held in pre-trial detention also dropped 13 percent between 2011 and 2015, Clarke said.

In a report this year about the potential ramifications of raising the age in North Carolina, Jon Guze, a director of legal studies with the John Locke Foundation, a conservative think tank based in the state, cited research finding that recidivism rates are significantly lower when young offenders are pushed through the juvenile justice system.

Initially, funneling older teens into the juvenile justice system could mean incurring additional costs, from hiring more family court judges, juvenile prosecutors and public defenders to building more courts and detention facilities, said Krista Larson of the Vera Institute, a research organization that advocates for changes in the criminal justice system.

But, she said, "States that have raised the age have not seen their juvenile court systems crushed by the numbers." A 2011 Vera Institute study found that if North Carolina raised the age to 18, the state would save $52.3 million a year.

After Connecticut passed its "raise the age" law in 2007, the state ended up spending slightly less on its juvenile justice system than it did before the age was raised, according to the Justice Policy Institute.

Arrests of 15- to 19-year-olds decreased 60 percent between 2008 and 2015, according to data compiled by the state's Office of Policy and Management. The number of 16- and 17-year-olds in the adult prison population dropped by three-quarters between 2009 and 2016. The number of 18- to 21-year-old prisoners fell more than half.

"We can't prove cause and effect here," said Mike Lawlor, the state's undersecretary for criminal justice policy and planning who sponsored the 2007 bill when he was a Democratic state lawmaker. "But you could theorize that if youth are being handled differently, then fewer and fewer are ending up in prisons as adults down the road."

Haggling in New York

New York's raise-the-age law is complicated, the result of years of haggling from both sides of the aisle.

The legislation ensures young people who commit nonviolent crimes will receive intervention and treatment. Young people will no longer be held at the notorious Rikers Island prison complex after October 2018. And people of all ages who have been crime-free for 10 years can now apply to have their criminal records sealed.

All misdemeanors will be automatically referred to family court, which handles juvenile cases. Youth charged with felonies will be treated a little differently. Their cases will be heard in a special part of adult criminal court where a family court judge will preside. No youth will be housed in adult prison facilities or jails.

"Is it the law that I would've written? No. But it's a political process," Ginsburg of the Legal Aid Society said. "The vast majority of the kids will be out of the adult system. It's a strong first step. But there's certainly more work to be done."

EVALUATING THE AUTHOR'S ARGUMENTS:

Viewpoint author Teresa Wiltz provides statistics that back trends toward rehabilitation and treatment of juveniles rather than imprisonment. But she is not one sided in her presenting of the facts and outside opinions. How does she provide balance while also conveying her argument?

Teens Are Not the Same as Adults

Lorelei Laird

"The juvenile justice reform movement is now bipartisan, with right-leaning organizations working with children's rights advocates."

In the following excerpted viewpoint, Lorelei Laird focuses on one case and uses interviews to examine the growing number of states that have raised the age for adult prosecution to eighteen. Laird describes the traumatic experiences of youths who are confronted with veteran and sometimes brutal adult criminals in prison to bring an understanding of the emotional and mental mountain kids in jail must climb to become rehabilitated. The author argues that while the focus should always be on rehabilitation, especially among youthful offenders ages eighteen to twenty-five, the trend toward raising the age for adult prosecution is a positive step. Laird is a legal affairs writer for the *ABA Journal*.

AS YOU READ, CONSIDER THE FOLLOWING QUESTIONS:

1. Should the age for adult prosecution be the same throughout the United States, or should it be determined by individual states?
2. How is the "beast mentality" described in the viewpoint?
3. How has behavioral science changed thinking about juvenile imprisonment and rehabilitation in recent years?

Teens sentenced to adult prison learn to adapt to an environment that can perpetuate criminal behavior.

Miguel Moll had a choice: Would he be a beast or a victim? Moll was 17 when he was taken into custody on suspicion of joyriding. He'd been a passenger in a stolen car. It was exactly the kind of dumb thing teenagers do; but under Texas law, 17-year-olds are automatically prosecuted as adults. He was booked into Harris County Jail in Houston with adult offenders.

Moll, who remembers weighing about 120 pounds and standing about 5 feet 9 inches at the time, was being taken to a holding cell, when a big man ran up to the bars and yelled, "I got this one!" That's when he made his choice.

"I became a beast just like them, in order to keep the other beasts off of me," Moll, now 45, testified to the Texas state legislature in 2015. "What choices did I have? I either submit, bow down or fight back. And at 17 years old, these things stick with you."

It stuck with Moll so well that he left jail with that "beast mentality"—and was quickly rearrested. This time, he ended up serving 19 years of a 20-year sentence for robbery in an adult prison. Testifying before the Texas legislature's Juvenile Justice & Family

Issues Committee, he said that because the adult system had no rehabilitation services—unlike juvenile detention, where those services are standard—he had to choose to reform himself.

Recalling it now, Moll says he realized less than halfway through his sentence that his tendency to fight with prison authorities, even when they were clearly abusing their power, could add time to his sentence. Rather than fighting with corrections officers, he says, he started fighting to change the culture of violence he saw.

"I was in there all those years, and I saw guys that were stuck in the same place where they [were when they] came in," he says. "So I knew that if I wanted to avoid the revolving door, then I had to do something."

Moll now works for Safe Hands Family and Children Programs, a Dallas-area nonprofit serving low-income families, and he is raising a son and working on a sociology degree. He also co-founded Hyped About HYPE (Helping Young People Excel), an organization that speaks to kids in the juvenile justice system about making better choices. He was speaking to the legislature on behalf of that group, along with three other men, in support of a bill intended to raise the age of adult jurisdiction in Texas to 18.

That bill—sponsored by Rep. Ruth Jones McClendon, D-San Antonio—failed, as did two similar bills. But increasingly, that makes Texas an outlier. Since 2009, seven states have raised the age of adult prosecution to 18, and five more tried during their 2015–2016 legislative sessions. In 2017, advocates are expecting "raise the age" bills in at least five states—more if you count proposals to increase the age to 21.

These aren't bleeding-heart liberal states; one of the early adopters was reliably conservative Mississippi. In fact, the juvenile justice reform movement is now bipartisan, with right-leaning organizations working with children's rights advocates. They're responding to studies showing that adult penalties lead to more teen recidivism, new science showing teenage brains really do mature later, and increasing political and financial pressure to address high incarceration rates.

Though not everyone is on board—law and order concerns and financial worries have stalled reform in some statehouses—advocates for juveniles say it's definitely a trend.

"We're at a critical time right now," says Marcy Mistrett, CEO of the Campaign for Youth Justice, a Washington, D.C.–based national initiative focused on ending adult prosecution for juveniles. "We now have the fewest states left in history—seven—that define criminal responsibility younger than 18. I believe that this is a fight we can win."

Second Chances

While Moll was learning the dubious lessons of adult prison, Charleston White was learning some very different things in Texas juvenile detention.

White wasn't an obvious candidate for rehabilitation. At 14, he joined a group of teens who tried to rob a Foot Locker and ended up killing a man. Though White wasn't the one who pulled the trigger, he was convicted of murder for his involvement. Testifying to the state legislature, he said he became a gang leader in juvenile detention. The state had the option to send him to adult prison when he turned 18, and he wanted to go. Growing up, he'd seen so many men from his community go to prison that he "literally believed that going to prison is what made you a man," he said.

But four adult "house parents"—corrections officers who White says acted like parents to him—saw through White's tough facade. He says they drove more than three hours to Fort Worth to tell a judge that White should stay in the juvenile system, risking their jobs in doing so.

Reflecting on it now, White says his attitude changed instantly. "I wanted to go back and be accepted by my friends, because I feared their rejection, but I also now have something inside of me that's pulling me in a different direction," says White, who co-founded Hyped About HYPE with Moll. "Because I don't want to disappoint these people. … Now somebody finally believed in me other than my mother."

And it's a good thing they did because programs in juvenile detention helped him understand his own thoughts, feelings and actions and gave him empathy for others. None of those programs would have been available in adult prison. It made him, he says, who he is today—a juvenile justice and community activist who's worked with the White House, a proud father and a student who hopes to eventually earn a law degree.

This kind of second chance was the original goal of juvenile justice. The first juvenile court was established in 1899 in Chicago by Progressive Era reformers who objected to the practice of putting kids in adult jails next to hardened criminals. They believed young people, if put through a system with more benign influences, could be rehabilitated.

Those juvenile systems had their ups and downs, but they met a serious challenge in the 1990s when crime rates rose and public concern grew about minors breaking the law. Over that decade, 45 states passed some kind of law that made it easier to try juveniles as adults, according to research from the John D. and Catherine T. MacArthur Foundation.

"It was a period of heightened moral panic," says Laurie Garduque, director of justice reform at the foundation, which is wrapping up a 20-year program supporting juvenile justice research and reforms. "There was a sense that the juvenile justice system was not able to deal with these 'more serious offenders' [or] 'superpredators,' as they were labeled."

But 20 years later, states are starting to rethink that. An important reason for that, child advocates say, is that the US Supreme Court has led the way with a series of important decisions on juvenile justice. Beginning in 2005 and continuing up to the 2015–2016 term, the Supreme Court has held that it's unconstitutional to execute people for crimes they committed as juveniles; outlawed automatic life without parole for nonhomicide crimes committed by juveniles; extended that ruling to homicide crimes; and, in 2016, made the ban on life sentences retroactive.

The Teen Brain Difference

Marsha Levick, deputy director and chief counsel of the Juvenile Law Center in Philadelphia, says that helped start a conversation about how "kids are different." And that conversation, she says, is partly because advances in behavioral and brain science show that adolescent brains really are different.

As Dr. Judith Edersheim, co-director of the Center for Law, Brain and Behavior at the Massachusetts General Hospital, explains it, there are three widely agreed-upon differences between adult brains and adolescent brains. One is that during adolescence, kids actually lose "gray matter," the brain cells that do all of the brain's computation. This "pruning" of gray matter is especially concentrated in the frontal lobes, which are responsible for self-control, planning, decision-making and other executive functions.

At the same time, Edersheim says, teenagers get more "white matter," the cells that pass messages between parts of the brain, which increases processing speed. Scientists think these two changes make the brain more efficient, even though it also loses some computational ability. This process of brain maturation continues after the body matures; some scientists think it ends as late as age 25.

But perhaps the most conspicuous difference, Edersheim says, is that adolescent brains have more circulating dopamine—a neutrotransmitter that scientists believe governs rewards and learning—and more receptors in their brains to pick it up. Dopamine is released when a person receives many kinds of rewards, including new experiences, as well as things such as food and sex. This predisposes teenagers to seek out rewards and novelty.

The thinking, Edersheim says, is that this helps push adolescents out of the nest and into the world. And what kids learn during this process, she says, helps determine what parts of the gray matter get pruned. That means a kid's environment matters a lot, and adult prison isn't the best environment.

"If you don't provide an adolescent with an opportunity to develop a social competency or self-esteem, if you don't put them in contact with pro-social peers, then you're setting trajectories which actually might persist through adulthood," Edersheim says. "Adolescents are really these neurologic sponges for their environment."

That's the science that's helping fuel the "kids are different" conversation Levick mentions. But at the same time, Levick says, that conversation is being driven by another discussion the country is having about justice reform generally. And that's very much a bipartisan conversation.

"Conservatives were the ones who stepped forward most recently and said, 'This is becoming fiscally irresponsible, to take what are now increasingly limited public resources and … lock up a population that doesn't really pose a safety risk,'" says Levick, who co-founded the Juvenile Law Center in 1975. "And I think once conservatives began putting that message out there, liberals and progressives were more than happy to join in."

Dianna Muldrow, a policy analyst at the conservative policy organization Right on Crime, says it's about more than money—it's about creating better outcomes, for society as well as for teenagers. Three decades of research have consistently shown higher recidivism rates for teenagers sent to adult prison. For example, a 2007 review of studies by the Centers for Disease Control and Prevention found that the kids who served time in adult prison were 34 percent more likely to commit new crimes than similar kids who went to juvenile detention.

Outcomes for the kids themselves are also bad. According to the Campaign for Youth Justice, which used Department of Justice and CDC numbers, teens under 18 being held in adult jails are 19 times more likely to commit suicide than teens generally, and 36 times more likely than those held in juvenile facilities. The Bureau of Justice Statistics says youths under 18 were 21 percent of those sexually assaulted in adult jails in 2005, despite being only 1 percent of jail inmates that year.

Muldrow also notes that when teens are treated as adults, there's no requirement for the police to notify the parents. Treating kids as kids helps keep their parents involved.

In some facilities, sexual assault is addressed by putting the youngest inmates in solitary confinement—a practice that quickly and catastrophically hurts their mental health, driving up suicide rates. In 2016, President Barack Obama banned solitary confinement for juveniles in federal prison, saying it's overused and can have devastating, lifelong consequences. And these are kids who often already have problems. Kids who get in legal trouble have disproportionately suffered abuse, neglect or another trauma. A DOJ study found that 50 to 70 percent have behavioral health diagnoses.

And kids of color make up a disproportionate number of those treated as adults, reflecting a racial disparity trend in other parts of the criminal justice system. The Campaign for Youth Justice says black adolescents are nine times more likely to be sentenced as adults compared to their white contemporaries; Latino juveniles are 40 percent more likely; and American Indian youths are nearly twice as likely. A federally funded 2007 study of juvenile justice in three cities said that while some of this can be explained by nonracial risk factors—such as family income, the age of the mother at the time of her first birth and education problems—that didn't entirely eliminate the disproportionate numbers.

Garduque says much of the behavioral research was already available in the 1990s, when states were passing laws that treated teenagers more like adults. But nobody had set out the legal implications of that research, she says, which was part of why the MacArthur Foundation spent two decades funding that kind of work. And the Supreme Court rulings, which relied in part on MacArthur-funded research, set the precedent.

"This idea that children are different for the purposes of criminal punishment has now become a powerful constitutional principle," Garduque says.

EVALUATING THE AUTHOR'S ARGUMENTS:

Does viewpoint author Lorelei Laird use president Barack Obama's ban on solitary confinement for imprisoned juveniles as evidence that the problem of juvenile justice has reached the top levels of the American government? Explain your reasoning.

Victim Rights Should Not Be Lost in the Juvenile Incarceration Debate

National Organization of Victims of Juvenile Murderers

"Victims, cases, and states differ, and we support all victims' family members to express their own views."

In the following viewpoint, the National Organization of Victims of Juvenile Murderers (NOVJM) argues that though each individual case is different, many juveniles who commit violent crimes are culpable enough to be held responsible. Some minors who commit murder may be evaluated as being a long-term danger to public safety and demonstrate an irreversible disregard for the value of human life. The authors also contend that the amount of research and debate that have resulted in current laws should not be underestimated. The NOVJM, formerly the NOVJL, is an organization that supports victims' rights and truth telling about the facts of the cases and asks that victims not be unnecessarily retraumatized in the process.

"At What Age Can We Hold Juveniles Criminally Responsible?" National Organization of Victims of Juvenile Murderers (www.teenkillers.org). Reprinted by permission.

AS YOU READ, CONSIDER THE FOLLOWING QUESTIONS:
1. Should victim families have any say in the sentencing of youth murderers?
2. Has enough been done to consider the feelings of the families of victims?
3. Are some crimes so heinous that they justify life sentences for juveniles?

NOVJL has devoted this website primarily to remembering our murdered loved ones and advocating for victims rights, and we have tried to avoid getting specific about what we think the specific laws should be regarding juvenile offender sentencing. Victims, cases, and states differ, and we support all victims' family members to express their own views on how they feel in their individual cases. Laws and sentencing are for our courts, legislatures, and citizens as a whole to decide. One of the more troubling specifics that our society has to sift through is the question of what age a person becomes old enough to be held criminally culpable as an adult.

Bright Lines

States define adulthood criminally in different ways. Most draw a line at 18, some states 17 and even 16. Some differ depending on if the crime was a felony or a misdemeanor, violent or non-violent. One of the questions in this public policy debate about juvenile offender sentencing that continues to plague us all is where to draw those "bright lines" in the law.

For example, at 18 not everyone is smart enough to cast an educated vote, and at 16 not everyone is mature enough to drive, and at 65 not everyone is ready to retire. But the law draws "bright lines" because it really has to—we have no choice in our society sometimes. We have to set averages that can be broadly applied, knowing that at times those bright lines will be wildly inappropriate to the individual case.

Would your stance on juvenile incarceration change if you or someone you loved were the victim of a crime perpetrated by a minor?

On our Offender Page we discuss further this issue of adolescent, juvenile, adult, and how the law generally sees these points.

On our Research and the Brain page we share some important psychological and neurological research, including the all important focus on what the brain science actually says and how it has been horribly misinterpreted by offender advocates, and to a certain extent, wrongly bought into by some courts.

Sophisticated Thinking About a Complex Issue

But here, inspired by an article in the *Seattle Times* called "Right From Wrong—At What Age Do Children Develop a Moral Sense, And Understand What It Means To Commit A Crime?" we decided to add thoughtfully to this complicated question—where SHOULD we draw the line on ages for young people when they are committing seriously violent crimes?

The *Seattle Times* article supports information encouraging to both "sides" in this debate: offender advocates who want to end long sentences for teen killers; and to people like us who care deeply about public and personal safety and recognize, quite factually and realistically, that some people even at a younger age could be so irretrievably dangerous that they cannot be allowed to ever walk among us again. This gives the article even more credibility—because it does not take sides, it does put forward best data-driven thinking by experts in the juvenile field.

Read the whole article for yourself. We certainly do not disagree with its emphasis on rehabilitating most juvenile offenders and the need to treat most juveniles in their own criminal justice system. But after interviewing experts in pediatrics, juvenile medicine, psychology, juvenile rehabilitation, and child psychiatry here are some highlights worth noting in this discussion:

- "Above all, their message was this: chronological age means nothing. ... It is typical that children charged with crimes are not functioning at their chronological ages"—we know this means that juvenile offenders can be both more culpable and less culpable than some of their peers, depending.
- Juveniles must be "held accountable for their behavior ... [and] there are some who are not of adult legal age who probably need to have pretty long sentences because they have done horrendous crimes, a lot of them. ..."
- Killing someone is a "psychological turning event" even for a young person that makes them much harder to rehabilitate.
- Child Psychiatrist Dr William Womack says, "The things that lead a kid to not care if they kill someone make it hard for them to be part of society. They don't look at human life as being very valuable."

Developmental experts offered this:

- "By age 6, normal children are developing an internal conscience. 'They have a pretty good sense, inside themselves, of what they're supposed to do; and if they do something wrong, bells go off for them,' Womack says."
- "By age 9 or 10 they grasp the idea that we have to have rules so people can get along, and we don't have chaos."

- "Ages 12 and 13 tend to be a transitional, awkward period. … However, if they're involved with a gang where they have to go through initiation, for example, they are often very independent and streetwise at an early age—11, or even younger."
- Cognitive function develops from "concrete" to "abstract" in the middle teen years, usually between 12 and 15. "That's where a person becomes able to understand the consequences of their behavior or actions."
- Most experts follow Piaget's theories that the brain changes to allow more abstract and future-oriented thought during these middle years.
- What science tells us pretty clearly is that we must evaluate juvenile culpability on a case by case basis.
- Dr James Farrow, Associate Professor of Medicine and Pediatrics at University of Washington School of Medicine, says a good general line is age 14 where before that time "a kid will be clearly less mature in terms of brain functioning … over 14, you might be able to make the case that they should be thinking like an adult."
- Farrow cites the "mature minor" doctrine that allows people at age 14 to consent to their own medical treatment such as mental health, substance abuse, pregnancy, etc.
- At 14 or 15 people begin to "look at the complexity of rightness and wrongness."
- The capacity to think about the complexity of morality takes place fairly early in adolescence—"as early as 11 or 12 with some children—and commonly by 14 to 17."

We note with interest at this point that the LAWS in all 50 of the United States reflect exactly the age ranges and observations of these experts!

The article goes on to stress how maturity and culpability varies widely from individual to individual, and that often capacity for morality does not mean that they have been "taught" properly. Another interesting point is how younger adolescents sometimes have "magical thinking" that nothing will happen to them if they do something bad. The experts recommend that "powerful penalties" for offenders under age 14 are not meaningful as deterrents because going to prison for the rest of their lives is not something they can "compute … they feel invulnerable."

History Always Provides Important Context

We have discussed elsewhere on this website about what we learned from history … that up until the Industrial Revolution adolescence did NOT exist for most of human history in ALL cultures. Life spans were shorter. All people went into marriage and family rearing on their own soon after puberty. Ritual initiation into adulthood in all religions and cultures took place around 13 or so. Young people passed almost immediately from child to adult—with nothing in between.

The economic competition of the industrial era made it necessary to delay entry into adulthood and create the artificial construct of adolescence because in factories young people could work just as well, and cheaper than older people. 30 year olds did not want to compete for a factory job with a 14 year old, medicine was getting better, and educational opportunities expanded with the printing press, creating better and longer schooling experiences that also helped to keep young people out of the job market longer.

And the field of Anthropology has been very instructive on this question—we are the ONLY species with such long childhoods! Even long-lived and high functioning species like chimpanzees kick the young one out on their own by ages 3–5. There are many psychologists who think the now two-plus decades that our species keeps hold on our young people has actually become significantly dysfunctional and problematic not only for our young, but for us all.

The Laws Today

The more we take in the breadth of expertise on this issue, the more we are convinced that the laws in most state are pretty much right on target. Few in the general public really have an appreciation for how much careful thought and debate, hard work and expertise, compromise, principle and leadership goes into wrestling a policy into a state law. When considering the sum whole of all 50 states, all 50 state legislatures, the US Congress, and the many, many very capable people who contribute to how our laws are made, we see that the system has actually made some very good decisions and drawn some very well-considered lines.

All states and the federal government have come to these same conclusions: Older juveniles can be held criminally responsible in some cases. Some people are hopelessly, defectively dangerous even at a very young age. Most juveniles deserve a real chance at rehabilitation for most crimes. Exceptionally violent crime changes young people into people that are very hard to allow out in society for a very, very long time. Ages 14–17 are reasonable ages for consideration for trial in the adult criminal justice system—on a case by case basis— because the juvenile system releases offenders after only a few years at 21 who are still very dangerous in some cases.

Prosecutors who we elect get to exercise tremendous discretion about how to charge cases. Judges get to make significant decisions about how criminal cases proceed. Every offender is represented by legal defense. They get appeals after conviction. They get usually years to prepare their cases before trial. They get to make many motions and argue evidence. They get to make the case for receiving a lesser sentence at many points in the system.

Overall, the system really HAS worked well, really has drawn some very correct lines, and that is why we at NOVJL sometimes find the rhetoric and propaganda from offender advocates to be at times particularly simplistic, shallow, and uncaring about the well-being of those at risk from certain dangerous teens.

Some of those working against the prison sentences being served by those who murdered our loved ones just repeat the same "its a human rights violation to imprison a juvenile" no matter their crime, no matter their age, if they are under 18.

Sadly we know that the major human rights violations in this discussion were the ones suffered by our murdered loved ones at the hands of their killers. Murder—the ultimate human rights violation.

Since we have found that many of these advocates would not be in this fight without the funding streams that support it, we have grown weary of their unwillingness to see the discussion about "bright lines" in the law with the breadth with which we have learned to view it.

EVALUATING THE AUTHORS' ARGUMENTS:

Did the viewpoint authors represent the families of murder victims fairly? How did they achieve or fail at this while also debating the larger point?

At What Age Are We Responsible for Our Own Actions?

"The law, and the people who write and interpret it, are just as befuddled about how to handle this situation as any anxious parent."

Alan Greenblatt

In the following excerpted viewpoint, Alan Greenblatt asserts the impossibility of creating a one-size-fits-all policy for juvenile offenders in the United States. Citing historical precedence and a range of different issues facing a wide variety of youth in America, Greenblatt contends that each case should be judged individually, with a focus on understanding that kids in many of our communities often do not boast the maturity level to be deemed responsible for their actions. Because their brains are not fully developed, teens often lack strong decision-making ability. Greenblatt is a staff writer for Governing, a media platform for state and local government leaders.

"What Is the Age of Responsibility?" by Alan Greenblatt, Governing Institute, September 30, 2009. Reprinted by permission.

1. Is there a specific age of responsibility, or does it vary based on individuals and their life circumstances?
2. How could rehabilitating rather than jailing youthful lawbreakers positively impact society?
3. Would easier access to college for poor kids reduce the crime rate?

Justin McNaull grew up in a hurry. By the time he was 23, McNaull had graduated from college, married and gone to work for his local police force in Virginia. But McNaull, now 36, still bristles at the memory of something he wasn't allowed to do at 23: go down to the airport counter and rent a car. "I'd been involved in police pursuits at more than 100 mph," he says, "and yet they still wouldn't rent me a car."

To many young people, rental-car restrictions are more than an annoyance. They're also a confusing contradiction, in terms of what society expects of them. After all, states trust people to drive at a much younger age: Most states issue driver's licenses to persons as young as 16 years old. Yet nearly a decade must pass before the same persons can earn the trust of Hertz or Avis.

By the time adolescents become adults, they are accustomed to such inconsistent treatment. Practically from puberty, young people are bombarded with mixed signals about the scope of their rights and the depth of their responsibilities. And most of those mixed signals come from the laws of state and local governments. In most respects, people are considered adults at 18. That's when they can vote and enter into legal contracts—including the purchase, if not rental, of a car. But a 20-year-old Marine, just back from patrolling the streets of Baghdad, would have to turn 21 before he could join a local police force in most cities in the United States. A 20-year-old college junior, far more educated than the average American, cannot buy alcohol or enter a casino. In 10 states, a single 20-year-old cannot legally have sex with a 17-year old. But in nearly every state, a 16-year-old can marry—if he has his parents' permission. (A handful of states allow girls to marry before boys.)

Teens often receive mixed messages regarding responsibility.

The most glaring examples lie within the criminal justice system. A spike in juvenile violence two decades ago spurred state legislators to adopt the mantra "adult time for adult crimes." Consequently, in most states, a 10-year-old charged with murder can be tried as an adult. Slightly older teens can be tried in adult courts for virtually every other crime. Even when states wait until 18 to treat criminals as adults, they don't like to wait long. Until recently, inmates at youth detention facilities in New Mexico were woken up just one minute after midnight on their 18th birthdays, in order to be moved to adult prisons.

Recently, many of these lines drawn between adolescence and maturity have been called into question. For example, the presidents of 135 universities are campaigning to consider lowering the drinking age from 21. They note that binge drinking on campus is rampant despite the stricture and argue that if students were given the right to drink at an earlier age, they might handle it more responsibly. Another argument is a reprise of the one that came up 40 years ago when servicemen came home from Vietnam. Then, the complaint was that soldiers were old enough to die but not to vote. (The 26th Amendment took care of that problem by lowering the voting age to 18.) Today, military personnel returning from Iraq and Afghanistan are left to question why they can fight America's wars but still can't patronize its bars.

Meanwhile, legislatures and courts are hearing a very different argument from a group of people that haven't traditionally testified before them: neuroscientists. Using advanced brain-scanning technology, scientists are getting a better view of how the human brain develops than ever before. And what they've found is that in most people, the prefrontal cortex and its links to other regions of the brain are not fully formed until age 25—much later than anyone had realized. These areas are the seat of "executive decision making"—the parts of the brain that allow people to think through the likely consequences of an action, weigh the risks and benefits and stop themselves from acting on impulse. In other words, the stuff that makes you a mature person.

To state and local lawmakers and judges, the brain research can come as a revelation: Maybe the car-rental companies were right all along. What to do about this is another matter. In America, "adulthood" already has its familiar compass points, 18 and 21. But what is the age of responsibility? And what if that age—the point when citizens are responsible enough to earn all of the rights a democracy confers upon its people—bears no resemblance to the ages already enshrined in law? Finding the answers to those questions is a more complicated task than simply choosing a milestone birthday. "There's been a growing recognition that most of our earlier law in how we treat adolescents and young adults was chaotic and not tied to any empirical rationale," says Brian Wilcox, a psychologist at the University of Nebraska. "When many of these laws were established, there really wasn't research on which they could be based."

The age at which children are considered mature is rooted in a mix of culture, convenience and historical precedent. Aristotle wrote of 21 as the age when a person would have completed three 7-year stages of youth development. During the Middle Ages, legend has it that 21 was considered the age of adulthood because that's when men were capable of wearing a full suit of armor. Arbitrary as such reasoning may sound to modern Americans, 21 stuck as a threshold age through the 19th century and into the 20th. Until they turned 21, young people owed their parents either their labor or their wages, whether that meant working on the family farm or operating a machine in an urban factory and handing over their pay.

But during the Progressive Era, reform efforts and adolescent research began to change notions about growing up. States, and eventually the federal government, enacted child-labor laws, keeping kids from working and ultimately making their attendance in high school compulsory. Such laws were opposed by business groups, which hated to let go of the cheap labor, and supported by unions, which didn't like the cheaper competition.

Through the middle of the 20th century, the onset of adulthood seemed to come earlier and earlier. War was partly responsible for that, as 18-year-olds went off to fight in World War II, followed by the wars in Korea and Vietnam. On the home front, manufacturing jobs didn't require a high-school diploma. It was thus common for 18-year-olds to support themselves and start their own families. And the rise of youth culture in the 1950s and 60s turned the teen years into their own distinctive stage of development—and consumer spending. There was a new sense that reaching the end of this life phase was a rite of passage in and of itself.

Nowadays, teens face more cultural pressure than ever to grow up fast, in certain ways. Recent controversies over whether 16-year-old pop star Miley Cyrus has sexualized her image is the latest symptom of that. Yet there's a strong pull in exactly the opposite direction, too. Many more 18-year-olds are choosing college over work now than a generation or two ago. They live independently at school for part of the year but under their parents' roofs for the rest. People are getting married later than they used to, and many have become slower about starting their own careers. Even before the current recession, plenty of college grads and dropouts had "boomeranged" back to Mom and Dad's house. Sociologists now talk of "extended adolescence" and "delayed adulthood."

That means that the window of time during which teens and young adults "grow up" is opening wider. This partly explains why state and local governments are so haphazard when it comes to young people: The law, and the people who write and interpret it, are just as befuddled about how to handle this situation as any anxious parent. Mostly, they have responded by cracking down. On an annual basis, the number of laws regulating the behavior of people under 18 has more than tripled since the 1950s. Curfews are now common. Recently, states have banned minors from purchasing items such as nitrous-oxide inhalants and fruit-flavored mini-cigars. Various jurisdictions have restricted "sexting"—sending lewd photos via cell phones. And 20 states ban only those under 18 from talking on cell phones while driving, despite evidence that the behavior (even using a hands-free device) is treacherous among drivers of all ages.

FAST FACT

All but three states had banned texting while driving by April 2018. Missouri was the only state to have outlawed it only for teen and novice drivers.

So there is a bit of hypocrisy, too, in the way governments define the age of responsibility. While nearly every state recently has put new limits on teen drivers, no state has begun restricting—or even testing—elderly drivers, some of whom may, like teens, lack mastery of their vehicles. Franklin Zimring, a UC Berkeley law professor, suggests that it's easier to block youngsters from obtaining rights than it is to take away rights to which adults have grown accustomed. That's because states aren't really denying young people rights, Zimring says. They're asking them to wait.

EVALUATING THE AUTHOR'S ARGUMENTS:

Does viewpoint author Alan Greenblatt assert that many juveniles in adult prisons committed crimes before they reached the age of responsibility with sufficient emphasis? Think about how this is effective or ineffective.

Facts About the Incarceration of Minors

Editor's note: These facts can be used in reports to add credibility when making important points or claims.

- About 250,000 juveniles are tried, sentenced, or jailed as adults every year across the United States.
- Approximately 7,500 American youths are locked up in prison cells on any given day.
- A majority of minors tried in adult courts have not committed serious or violent crimes.
- Youths of color are overwhelmingly represented among those who go through the juvenile justice system.
- All but 11 states allow or require youths charged as adults to be held in an adult prison.
- Nine states try all 16- and 17-year-olds as adults, regardless of the crime.
- Juveniles serving sentences in adult jails are 36 times more likely to commit suicide than those in youth facilities.
- The Centers for Disease Control and Prevention reports that youths moved from juvenile to adult prisons are 34 percent more likely to suffer from recidivism than those who stay in juvenile facilities.
- Nearly every state had adopted a juvenile justice system that revolved around treatment and prevention rather than punishment by 1925, but trends did not continue in that direction from that point forward.
- Every economic study has concluded that crime prevention and rehabilitation costs taxpayers far less than imprisonment.
- One report showed that intervention programs such as high school graduation programs can prevent as many as 250 crimes a year per $1 million spent, while spending the same amount for lockup facilities would prevent just 60 crimes per year.

- California and Florida spend more money on the prison system than they do higher education.
- The United States has the highest rate of youth confinement of any developed country in the world. In 2010, there were 173 youths for every 100,000 prisoners.
- The number of juvenile delinquency cases in the United States declined dramatically over the decade from 2004 forward.
- The juvenile offender population dropped nearly 50 percent from 2000 to 2012. The result was that in 2012 only one-fifth of juvenile facilities were at capacity or over capacity.
- About 1 in 10 incarcerated juveniles reported incidents of sexual victimization over a recent one-year period.
- Among the many issues faced by youths sentenced as adults upon release are adult criminal records, getting turned down for jobs, and denial of educational opportunities, including student financial aid.
- In 2013 about 10 percent of all violent crime in the United States was committed by youths. The FBI reported that those under 18 were targeted for less than 10 percent of all arrests.
- The number of arrests of juveniles dropped more than 50 percent from 2005 to 2014. That nearly quadrupled the rate of decrease of adult arrests, which stood at 14 percent.
- Violent crimes committed by those ages 12–17 dropped from 52 crimes per 100,000 youths in 1993 to just 9 per 100,000 youths in 2011.
- Research has concluded that the human brain does not fully develop until one's early twenties. Minors are more likely to engage in risky behavior without a full understanding of consequences and correct decision making in emotional situations until their brains are fully developed.
- In some states juveniles convicted in adult courts are required to serve their entire sentences in adult prisons.
- Most minors held in adult prisons have not committed serious offenses. About four-fifths are released before they reach 21 and almost all before their 25th birthday.
- Many adult lockups cannot ensure the safety of their juvenile prisoners without subjecting them to solitary confinement.

- Solitary confinement can be most harmful to juvenile prisoners emotionally and mentally. They are often locked up for 23 hours a day with no natural light.
- Two-thirds of imprisoned youths are saddled with one or more mental health conditions. But only about 40 percent receive any sort of mental health counseling.

Organizations to Contact

The editors have compiled the following list of organizations concerned with the issues debated in this book. The descriptions are derived from materials provided by the organizations. All have publications or information available for interested readers. The list was compiled on the date of publication of the present volume; the information provided here may change. Be aware that many organizations take several weeks or longer to respond to inquiries, so allow as much time as possible for the receipt of requested materials.

American Civil Liberties Union
125 Broad Street, 18th Floor
New York, NY 10004
(212) 549-2500
email: aclupreferences@aclu.org
website: www.aclu.org
The American Civil Liberties Union uses its resources to fight for and preserve individual rights and freedoms in the United States.

Annie E. Casey Foundation
701 St. Paul Street
Baltimore, MD 21202
(410) 547-6700
email: www.aecf.org/contact
website: www.aecf.org
The Annie E. Casey Foundation seeks to develop a better future for at-risk children of poor educational, economic, social, and health outcomes by strengthening families, building stronger communities, and providing access to opportunities.

Campaign for Youth Justice
1220 L Street NW, Suite 605
Washington, DC 20005
(202) 558-3580
email: info@cfyj.org
website: www.campaignforyouthjustice.org
Campaign for Youth Justice is a national program seeking to end the prosecution, sentencing, and imprisoning of youths under the age of eighteen in the adult justice system.

Center for Children's Law and Policy
1701 K Street NW, Suite 1100
Washington, DC 20006
(202) 637-0377
email: info@cclp,org
website: www.cclp.org
The Center for Children's Law and Policy aims to ensure that the response to juveniles who get into trouble with the law is developmentally appropriate and free of racial or ethnic bias. It also seeks to strengthen youths so they avoid further involvement with the justice system.

Children's Defense Fund
25 East Street NW
Washington, DC 20001
(202) 628-8787
email: cdfinfo@childrensdefense.org
website: www.childrensdefense.org
The Children's Defense Fund works to ensure a safe, healthy, and fair start to life for children through work with families and local communities while providing a strong and independent voice for youth rights.

Coalition for Juvenile Justice

1319 F Street NW, Suite 402
Washington, DC 20004
(202) 467-0864
email: info@juvjustice.org
website: www.juvjustice.org
The Coalition for Juvenile Justice works to ensure that fewer youths are at risk of delinquency and become involved with the justice system.

Justice for Families

1913 Azalea Street
Sulphur, LA 70663
(443) 418-5201
email: info@justice4families.org
website: www.justice4families.org
The mission of Justice for Families is to halt the spread of juvenile incarceration and work with youths and their families to create better lives.

Sentencing Project

1705 DeSales Street NW, 8th Floor
Washington, DC 20036
(202) 628-0871
email: staff@sentencingproject.org
website: www.sentencingproject.org
The Sentencing Project has worked toward a fair and effective American criminal justice system since 1986 by promoting reforms in sentencing policy based on unjust racial disparities and practices.

For Further Reading

Books

Kristen A. Bates and Richelle S. Swan, *Juvenile Delinquency in a Diverse Society*. Washington, DC: Sage Publications, 2017.

> The authors seek to provide a fresh perspective and examination of juvenile delinquency and social policies. They cite many factors that control youth criminality, including race, ethnicity, class, gender, and sexual orientation.

Nell Bernstein, *Burning Down the House: The End of Juvenile Prison*. New York, NY: New Press, 2016.

> This author takes a radical approach to juvenile justice through her investigative work, concluding that there is no good way to lock up a child. The author advocates that state-run detention centers should be abolished.

Preston Elrod and L. Scott Ryder, *Juvenile Justice: A Social, Historical, and Legal Perspective*. Burlington, MA: Jones & Bartlett Learning, 2013.

> Two experts on juvenile justice write about the effectiveness of the system in theory and through an historical perspective. Included are the development of the juvenile court in the United States and chapters on status and violent offenders.

Karen M. Hess, *Juvenile Justice*. Boston, MA: Wadsworth Publishing, 2009.

> This book provides practical and complete information about the American juvenile justice system. It explores the process youths face, as well as prevention program through their schools and communities.

John Hubner, *Last Chance in Texas: The Redemption of Criminal Youth*. New York, NY: Random House, 2008.

> The author of this book focuses on one troubled youth while writing about the surprisingly successful treatment and rehabilitation program in Texas.

Edward Humes, *No Matter How Loud I Shout: A Year in the Life of Juvenile Court*. New York, NY: Simon & Schuster, 2015.

> This award-winning book examines the juvenile court system with a sense of urgency for those concerned with the future of American youth. It looks at how sentencing affects children for the rest of their lives.

Barry A. Krisberg, *Juvenile Justice: Redeeming Our Children*. Washington, DC: Sage Publications, 2004.

> The author debunks myths about juvenile justice in writing about how to achieve a fairer system that would protect at-risk children while building stronger and safer communities.

John T. Whitehead and Steven P. Lab, *Juvenile Justice: An Introduction*. New York, NY: Routledge, 2018.

> The two authors present a thorough picture of juvenile offending and delinquency theories, as well as research into successful interventions and treatments. They also provide suggestions on improving juvenile courts.

Periodicals and Internet Sources

Sarah Brown and Anne Teigen, "Rethinking Solitary Confinement for Juveniles," National Conference of State Legislatures, May 2016. http://www.ncsl.org/research/civil-and-criminal-justice/rethinking-solitary-confinement-for-juveniles.aspx.

Andrew R. Calderon, "A Dangerous Brain," Marshall Project, August 14, 2018. https://www.themarshallproject.org/2018/08/14/a-dangerous-brain?ref=collections.

Michelle Chen, "Our Criminal Courts Are Failing Juvenile Defendants," *Nation*, October 31, 2017. https://www.thenation.com/article/our-criminal-courts-are-failing-juvenile-defendants.

Cara H. Drinan, "Outraged by Kids in Cages? Look at Our Entire Juvenile Justice System," Huffington Post, June 24, 2018. https://www.huffingtonpost.com/entry/opinion-drinan-juvenile-justice_us_5b2d5673e4b00295f15c6b0f.

Mike Huckabee, "Why Conservatives Should Support Juvenile Justice Reform," AL.com, February 6, 2018. https://www.al.com/opinion /index.ssf/2018/02/why_conservatives_should_suppo.html.

Juvenile Law Center, "Youth in the Justice System: An Overview," 2018. https://jlc.org/youth-justice-system-overview.

Bryan Robinson, "2 Teens at Center of Juvenile Crime Debate," ABC News, March 9, 2018. https://abcnews.go.com/US /story?id=93887&page=1.

Nicole Scialabba, "Should Juveniles Be Charged as Adults in the Criminal Justice System?," American Bar Association, October 3, 2016. https://www.americanbar.org/groups/litigation/committees /childrens-rights/articles/2016/should-juveniles-be-charged -as-adults.

Elizabeth Seigle, "Improving Outcomes for Youth in the Juvenile Justice System," National League of Cities, March 1, 2017. https://www.nlc .org/article/improving-outcomes-for-youth-in-the-juvenile-justice -system.

Douglas Singleterry, "It's Time for Criminal Justice Reform to Focus on Young Adults," Hill, August 17, 2017. https://thehill.com/blogs/ pundits-blog/civil-rights/346975-its-time-for-criminal-justice-re- form-to-focus-on-young-adults.

Deborah Smith, "Women and Girls in the Justice System," National Center for State Courts, 2017. https://www.ncsc.org/sitecore /content/microsites/trends/home/Monthly-Trends-Articles/2017 /Women-and-Girls-in-the-Justice-System.aspx.

Carl Stoffers, "Juvenile Justice: Can Young Criminals Be Reformed? A Growing Number of States Think So—but Not Everyone Is Convinced," New York Times, December 11, 2017. https://upfront .scholastic.com/issues/2017-18/121117/juvenile-justice .html#1220L.

David S. Tanenhaus, "First Things First: Juvenile Justice Reform in Historical Context," William S. Boyd School of Law, 2013. https:// scholars.law.unlv.edu/cgi/viewcontent.cgi?article=2009&context =facpub.

Rob Waters, "Detention Facilities Have Become Warehouses for Mentally Disturbed Youth," Psychotherapy Networker, September 6,

2017. https://www.psychotherapynetworker.org/blog/details/1293 /confronting-a-broken-juvenile-justice-system.

Patrick Webb, "Are Youth of Color Benefiting from Juvenile Justice Reform?," Juvenile Justice Information Exchange, November 20, 2017. https://jjie.org/2017/11/20/are-youth-of-color-benefiting-from -juvenile-justice-reform.

Christopher Zoukis, "Counseling and Community Service over Incarceration for Juvenile Offenders," Huffington Post, December 23, 2016. https://www.huffingtonpost.com/entry/counseling-and -community-_b_13821392.

Websites

Juvenile Justice Geography, Practice, Policy and Statistics (jjgps.org)

This site tracks reforms being implemented in the juvenile justice system state-by-state. It provides news updates on how various states are dealing with the issue.

National Juvenile Justice Network (www.njjn.org)

This reform-promoting site sends readers to like-minded organizations throughout the United States. It also updates readers on important news about juvenile justice in America.

Office of Juvenile Justice and Delinquency Prevention (www.ojjdp.gov)

This site empowers youth and promotes accountability through resources, news articles, and other information on the subject. It also provides services for those interested.

Youth.gov (youth.gov/youth-topics/juvenile-justice)

Youth.gov provides a wide range of articles, programs, resources, and publications that allow young people to become familiar with all issues related to juvenile justice. It also features videos and podcasts.

Index

juvenile court system
  and bias against youth of
    color, 47, 91
  focus on environmental fac-
    tors, 48–49

K
Kagan, Elena, 72

L
Laird, Lorelei, 84–91
Lambe, Shauneen, 60–63
Larson, Krista, 82
Lawlor, Mike, 82
Levick, Marsha, 88–89, 90
Lohrmeyer, Kristopher, 75–76
Louisiana, 14
low-risk offenders vs. high-risk
  offenders, 37
Lucas County, Ohio, 68–69

M
Maconochie, 35–36
maturity, historical concept
  of, 103–104
McCarthy, Patrick, 65
McNaull, Justin, 101
Medina, Andrew, 75–76
Miller, Derrick, 75–76
Miller, Evan, 74–75
minors, incarcerated
  in adult prisons, 40–44,
    52–59, 81
  and adverse impact on fam-
    ilies, 50
  alternatives to, 11–16, 64–69
  and education, 42, 43

  and enabling of crime, 60–63
  falling rate of, 27
  and home life, 17–20
  impact of, on adult crimi-
    nality, 26
  and life sentences, 71–76
  overview of arguments, 7–9
  as people who need help, 31
  and public health, 45–51
  raising of minimum age,
    77–83, 84–91
  rate, in United States vs.
    other nations, 22–27
  recidivism rates, 58
  release rates, in adult
    prisons, 59
  and responsibility for own
    actions, 100–105
  sexual assault, in adult pris-
    ons, 42, 53–54, 55–56, 90
  in solitary confine-
    ment, 90–91
  solutions for preventing, in
    adult prisons, 50–51
  spending on, in United
    States, 23
  staff-to-inmate ratios in,
    55, 56, 57
  suicide rates for, in adult
    prisons, 43, 56, 90
  and victim rights, 92–99
Mistrett, Marcy, 87
Moll, Miguel, 85–86
Muldrow, Dianna, 90

N
National Institute of Justice, 7

National Organization of
    Victims of Juvenile Murderers
    (NOVJM), 92–99
National Prison Rape
    Elimination Commission, 42
New York, 43–44, 79, 82–83
North Carolina, 79, 82

O
Öberg, Nils, 30, 31–32

P
Parker, Alison, 73
Pennsylvania, 12–13
Piquero, Alex, 11–16
Prison Rape Elimination Act
    (PREA, 2003), 42, 54–55
psychotherapy, 36–37

S
"Safely Home" (Youth Advocate
    Programs), 67, 68
Seattle Times, 94–95
sexual assault, 42, 53–54,
    55–56, 90
Shields, Derrick, 74
solitary confinement, 90–91
Steinberg, Laurence, 11–16
Stevenson, Bryan, 73
substance abuse, 19–20
suicide, 43, 56, 90
surveys
    educational/vocational services
        in prisons, 42
    rehabilitation vs. incarcera-
        tion, 12–16
Sweden, 29–32

T
Task Force on Community
    Preventive Services, 57–58
Texas, 44, 85–86

U
United Kingdom, 31, 32, 61–63

V
Vera Institute, 82
Vermont, 79
victim rights, 92–99

W
Washington State, 13
White, Charleston, 87
Wilcox, Brian, 103
Willow, Carolyne, 63
Wiltz, Teresa, 77–83
Womack, William, 95
Wood, Andrea, 52–59

Z
Zimring, Franklin, 105

Picture Credits

Cover Francis Demange/Gamma-Rapho/Getty Images; p. 10 Christian Science Monitor/Getty Images; p. 15 Andrew Lichtenstein/ Corbis News/Getty Images; pp. 19, 24, 66 ©AP Images; p. 30 Alain Le Garsmeur/Alamy Stock Photo; p. 35 Barcroft Media/Getty Images; p. 39 Mikael Karlsson/Alamy Stock Photo; p. 41 LightField Studios/ Shutterstock.com; p. 46 Steven Puetzer/Photographer's Choice/Getty Images; p. 54 Skyward Kick Productions/Shutterstock.com; p. 61 Digital First Media/Orange County Register via Getty Images; p. 70 josefkubes/Shutterstock.com; p. 72 Brandon Bourdages/Shutterstock .com; p. 78 Radius Images/Alamy Stock Photo; p. 85 Mark Boster/ The Los Angeles Times/Getty Images; p. 94 Tunatura/Shutterstock .com; p. 102 Monkey Business Images/Shutterstock.com.